THE SUNDAY TIMES

WITHDRAWN

Managing Change

Patrick Forsyth

D0161997

KoganPage

LONDON   PHILADELPHIA   NEW DELHI

First published in Great Britain and the United States in 2012 by Kogan Page Limited

120 Pentonville Road	1518 Walnut Street, Suite 1100	4737/23 Ansari Road
London N1 9JN	Philadelphia PA 19102	Daryaganj
United Kingdom	USA	New Delhi 110002
www.koganpage.com		India

© Patrick Forsyth, 2012

The right of Patrick Forsyth to be identified as the author of this work has been
asserted by him in accordance with the Copyright, Designs and Patents Act 1988.

ISBN	978 0 7494 6389 2
E-ISBN	978 0 7494 6390 8

British Library Cataloguing-in-Publication Data

A CIP record for this book is available from the British Library.

Library of Congress Cataloging-in-Publication Data

Forsyth, Patrick.
  Managing change / Patrick Forsyth.
    p. cm.
  ISBN 978-0-7494-6389-2 – ISBN 978-0-7494-6390-8   1. Organizational change–
Management.   I. Title.
  HD58.8.F677 2012
  658.4′06–dc23

                                                                      2011051471

Typeset by Graphicraft Ltd, Hong Kong
Printed and bound in India by Replika Press Pvt Ltd

Contents

Introduction: change – a synonym for success

Change is a good thing: it prevents stagnation, it prompts improvement and it links directly to the ongoing success of organisations – and of individuals. Are we all agreed on that? Change is good, right? Surely any aware and effective person would see this to be the case. In a much quoted phrase Gelett Burgess put it well: 'If in the last few years you haven't discarded a major opinion or acquired a new one, check your pulse. You may be dead.' Most people do not want to be characterised as a Luddite and they are in favour of the concept of change – right up to the moment someone walks up to their desk and says that there are going to be changes made *here*. Then most people's instinct is to be suspicious and defensive; they get ready for something negative and make ready to try to fend it off. Such attitudes make for a curious contradiction.

But change occurs; indeed it may need to be anticipated, prompted and certainly to be worked with and coped with when it is thrust upon us – and changes, positive changes, need to be made to work and work effectively if they are to move us forward. And in the early years of the twenty-first century this is the case perhaps more than ever before.

Change is the norm

In this introduction you will meet a quotation that could not be more apposite and is a fair maxim to take on board at the start of this review. That change must now be regarded as the norm is not just because of the general competitive nature of markets, and for that matter of the modern work environment, but also because every aspect of an organisation and its work can become more volatile following any particular economic upheaval. And as economic upheaval seems to have been much in evidence so far this century it would take a brave person to predict that the future will become suddenly more placid.

Let us be clear about this right at the start: change is going to be the norm for the foreseeable future. We can expect change to continue and for the pace of change to continue to increase. As Steve Case, Chairman, AOL Time Warner once said: 'There will be more confusion in the business world in the next decade than in any decade in history. And the current pace of change will only accelerate.' This comment will remain relevant for a good while and certainly such a situation affects everything that follows here.

Change may seem a fairly benign word, but it is almost normal for disaster to follow in its wake. Certain industries, like banking, once seemed stable, but they are as prone to difficulties as any other sector and have recently changed radically. Change can move us forward, but there can be casualties both corporate and personal along the way. So the process of change must be well handled to ensure that matters go smoothly and change works.

Examples of change

Consider first a couple of general examples of change; both show how changes can influence things radically in the long term:

1. Staff recruitment is a good example. Employment legislation has created much greater fairness but it has also made

recruitment far more difficult and time consuming to carry out. Sometimes the result is that recruiters play it safe or easy (hiring the best of a poor bunch of candidates rather than re-advertising perhaps) and make appointments they end up regretting. This leads to poor performance and difficulties while matters are sorted out: a negative result of changes which aimed to be positive. The same is true of dealing with poor performance. It can be such a complex process to dismiss someone that poor performance can continue for many months when in the long term it is in the interests of both employer and employee to make a prompt change.

2. Electronic communication is seen as a huge benefit. We are now in touch virtually instantly across the world and the advantages of this are legion; think how much more smoothly international customer relations runs now we have left telex and fax far behind. But there are downsides too. Emails tend to be written with insufficient thought and breakdowns in communications are more common as a result; and sometimes the damage done is considerable. Similarly, the absurd picture of people emailing to others in the office who are only a few metres away can be detrimental to ordinary communications, collaboration and understanding.

More specific examples that will give you greater understanding of the effect of change are as follows:

1. Defining the business

The thinking demonstrated here is an excellent example of how the most basic element of planning – just defining the business – can focus the mind, change a whole business and lead directly to new opportunities and growth.

Imagine a company, let us call them Scaffolding 'R Us, that rented out scaffolding. They defined their business very simply and directly as *the provision of scaffolding to the building trade*.

Just rethinking this took them through three stages, each of which resulted in distinct changes that had a positive effect on their business growth:

1. First, they replaced the description *building trade* with *construction industry*. This broadened the market to which they directed their marketing efforts, taking them into selling to companies constructing, for instance, motorway flyovers, or to oil rigs (where there is evidently copious amounts of scaffolding used) – effectively different markets and ones yielding potentially larger orders. A learning curve may have been necessary to deal with a different type of customer, but the business grew.
2. They then moved on and described their business less in terms of what they did, and more in terms of what it provided, in turn, for customers, so to *provide temporary access and support*. This took them into the leisure market, providing scaffolding to support seating at sports events and parades. Again new customers needed new approaches, but business expanded in this substantial sector.
3. Then they again refined the description, this time with more confidence, stressing *their skill and expertise in providing temporary access and support*. This, in turn, prompted them to enter export markets. Instead of erecting their scaffolding overseas (clearly shipping heavy steel poles is prohibitively costly), they ran training schools for local organisations and their staff in new markets, including the Middle East, where building was a rapid growth industry. This was a change that would never have been guessed at early on in the process.

Here change was created intentionally as an inherent part of an organisation's ongoing strategic planning. Such thinking can be very productive, and it is sometimes surprising how the status quo acts to blind an organisation to new opportunities when it only needs a fresh look and an open mind to spot some, and then to create significant and positive change.

2. An accurate basis of information

This example shows how change can creep up unobserved. It is illustrated by a personal recollection. I was working with a medium-sized firm of Chartered Accountants (with several offices spread across one UK county) and asked about their 'typical client'. The senior partner described a family business of a certain size and type (the details are unimportant). I asked what proportion of their clients fitted this category and was told it was 'about two-thirds'.

Subsequent analysis – done very simply – showed he had overestimated by twice the number; in fact only one-third of their clients fitted the description given. He was both out of date and had not troubled to check. Of the clients he *personally* handled, two-thirds *did* fit the description and up to a couple of years previously the proportion stated would have been correct across the firm. But times change.

This is not just a matter of getting a few numbers wrong. It really matters. In this firm decisions about marketing and promotion were being made on the assumption that the higher proportion was correct – and promotional materials were being designed largely for the wrong kind of people. Probably their effectiveness suffered as a result. Moral: planning, and the strategic decisions that follow it, *must be based on accurate information about what is happening.* Here a gradual change to the way the firm related to the market went unacknowledged and ultimately a rapid programme of change had to be put in place to reflect the actual situation.

3. A necessary skill

Change is necessary not only at the corporate level (for an organisation as a whole or a department or division of it) but also on a personal one. Again let me describe a personal situation. For some years I have listed writing alongside my work as a consultant and trainer. But when I was asked to write a book for the first time it was a real shock to the system. I did it and the book was duly published, but I realised that it was not as well written as it could have been. I had to change. I took a variety of actions to develop my writing skills and my next book was very much better. Having acquired a new, or upgraded, skill (albeit one that took further refinement) I was able to change my whole work pattern and found, especially some years later when I set up my own business, that my new work portfolio worked very well, both in terms of job satisfaction and convenience (I can write at home and only have to walk down one flight of stairs to my study), but also as a business activity. The process of doing this sort of writing changes too. I wrote my first book longhand (yes, it is a while ago!). For a long time now I could not have continued this work without a computer (and certain computer skills). Manuscripts are delivered by email, and increasingly the finished book or article is available to be read in electronic form (indeed this book is one of many of Kogan Page's titles now available for the Kindle and in other electronic book formats). Furthermore I recently wrote a book (on marketing) of which there is no paper copy; it is designed exclusively for sale over the internet by a specialist publisher (you can check it out on **www.quicklookbooks.com**). I was not the first and will certainly not be the last person to have to adapt to be able to do the job in hand or what I want to do: change is often necessary at a personal level (more of individual personal change in Chapter 6).

All these examples show the long-term and wide-ranging results of change and how downsides can occur even when positive change is the plan; the effects of every kind of change can be significant and perhaps radical. A manufacturer of fax machines may have had to change radically or go out of business when email became widespread and any organisation faced with a merger or takeover is going to spend some time getting used to change in every part of their operation. Clearly dealing with or making any change needs careful consideration.

So, with uncertainty being the order of the day, good implementation and management of change is essential and should smooth the path towards a continuing, if different, success.

Some people may hanker back to the 'good old days', but waiting for things to 'return to normal' is simply not one of the options. There are currently few, if any, safe havens, and few,

if any, organisations that offer a job for life and an adequate
and secure pension at the end. Change is now the norm in all
walks of life.

All sorts of factors contribute to the current nature of the
organisation and how it must operate. For example:

- **organisations are under greater market and financial
  pressures;**
- **changes in the way businesses and organisations now
  function (think of the IT revolution or international
  pressures, for instance);**
- **lower staff numbers and more pressure on individuals;**
- **reduced budgets and thus a reduced ability to fund
  personal or professional development;**
- **changed terms of employment and staff policies (think
  of how the pension schemes offered have changed in
  the past few years);**
- **technological development across a wide canvas;**
- **a general increase in both the amount and speed of
  change;**
- **the greater likelihood of having to make rapid change
  (and thus sometimes making changes without careful
  consideration).**

You can probably add to this list and events will certainly add to
it as time goes by. Therefore many managers and executives must
be able to deal with change and this leads us to consider two
overall areas:

1. Change must be an integral part of the way an organisation
   operates, yet little or none of it happens automatically.
   Essentially it is only individual people who can deal with
   this, make change occur and make it positive and effective.
2. Individuals must themselves be open to personal change;
   the only way forward may demand acquiring new skills,
   knowledge and attitudes and some of that may mean taking
   individual initiatives (because an employer will not do it
   all for you).

This book's message is addressed to the individual rather than the organisation or employer. It makes reference to the organisation, of course, and in any case it is the individual that influences the organisation, but the focus is on the individual and on individual action: on you and what you can do.

The book looks at change in the round: that is it is concerned with the process of change and what is formally called change management. However, it also considers other changes that may be necessary – large or small, personal or corporate – and how to view and deal with them. It looks at how *you* can instigate change, making it acceptable and effective. It shows how you can make what you do and how you do it successful; and how you can make the process continue being successful over time.

Action

At this stage it should be clear that you need to accept that change is part of your life, view it positively and particularly as something that you should actively seek and/or respond to in a way that takes you forward in a practical sense. Keep this in mind as you read the rest of this book.

1

The nature of change

While attitudes to change may be confused in some senses, as we saw in the introduction, the fact of change makes dealing with it a necessity not an option. No one can say that because change can be difficult they will 'simply stay as we are'. So if managing change is part of the current (and future) remit, then what makes it possible to embrace this and cope with it effectively? Perhaps the first thing is to recognise the nature of change: change is made necessary for a variety of reasons and comes in a variety of forms. Understanding why change may be necessary and also what can prompt unexpected change is the first step to anticipating, initiating or reacting to it.

The first categorisation that should be noted is essentially straightforward: changes can be prompted internally or externally. For example:

- **External factors may present threats (which some people prefer to dub challenges) that necessitate change (like a competitor taking action with which you must keep pace or aim to leapfrog), or may simply provide opportunities (for example, once computer** technology made it possible to access a whole address from a post code this was gradually taken up by more and more organisations aiming to improve customer service and/or contain costs).

- Internal factors where circumstances may necessitate change range from growth requiring a relocation of premises to a shortage of specialist qualified staff involving new ways of recruitment, training or processes.

It is clear even from the brief examples given so far that delay can make for difficulty. For example, customers might get impatient with an organisation demanding that they spell out their every contact detail when competitors can access them automatically in a few seconds. Such frustration could result in a changed image and lost business. So there is merit in being alert to such things and making sure that a broad, objective and regular review is part of the management process. As at every level – individual, departmental and corporate – the focus may need to be on the short term and on immediate activities; this may mean some specific steps need taking to make sure ongoing longer-term review happens. This may simply mean the inclusion of a dedicated 'change spotting' item on the agenda of departmental or board meetings. But it could also mean the adoption of more rigorous and prescribed action like the Japanese *kaizen* approach, which promotes gradual ongoing change. (See the box below for more detail of this philosophy; the principles described here in fact apply widely.)

Kaizen principles

Kaizen is a way of thinking and behaving. It provides guidelines to individuals and teams within an organisation, which it regards as something of a 'company family', and helps direct efforts towards achieving objectives as fully as possible. It makes change and improvement the concern of everyone – every employee is encouraged to consider initiatives that will help, improve customer service, eliminate waste, push costs down or increase profit. This involves 10 principles which give some indication of the scope of the overall approach. They are:

1. *A focus on customers:* because profit is only obtained outside the organisation, this is regarded as paramount and everyone has a personal responsibility to assist in this area.

2. *Making improvements continuously:* the aim is to create ongoing impact and a change is regarded as only existing until yet another way is discovered to make things better still.

3. *Acknowledging problems openly:* the aim is to miss out the typical denial stage regarding problems; as soon as something needs attention it is flagged and everyone is aware that change is necessary.

4. *Promoting openness:* this relates to communication and hierarchy; the more everyone is connected to everyone else the more cooperation is possible and the more easily change can occur.

5. *Creating work teams:* this goes beyond what is necessary operationally. Teams are regarded as creative (as with another Japanese originated technique, that of quality circles) and a network of formal and informal teams encourages cooperation.

6. *Cross functionality:* effort is made to override functional barriers to facilitate further cooperative thinking and problem solving.

7. *Harmony:* objectives are seen as a prime driver, and any friction is regarded as likely to restrict their achievement. The active avoidance of this at every level of interpersonal relationships is actively sought.

8. *Self-discipline:* this encompasses determination and focus on successfully addressing objectives and links to what in Western circles would probably be called empowerment. This too is seen as actively assisting and achieving ongoing change.
9. *Corporate-wide communication:* what some would see as obsessive communication, but regular, detailed and open communication is seen as essential to making the organisation work effectively and enable it to change as necessary.
10. *Enabling:* the fact that everyone is well informed must link to action; people are trained to see themselves as able, and indeed are expected to use their every experience to contribute to change and the success that flows from it.

Together all this makes *kaizen* a potent force within any organisation that embraces its principles. It becomes a significant part of culture and, because it drives improvement and particularly improvement focused on objectives, it is considered worth the effort it takes to initiate such a philosophy and make it work at a practical level.

If you need to know more then a good reference is Pat Wellington's book *Kaizen Strategies for Customer Care* (Pitman Publishing), which describes it well and links how it works to one clearly defined area to show its practicality.

The *kaizen* principles outlined above can of course be applied generally and on a less formal basis; even an individual can act on them to prompt change. For example, with regard to point 10, enabling, one major hotel group gives its staff exceptional individual authority. Someone handling a complaint not only deals with the guest and sorts it but also decides on and implements any action that may be necessary to make amends. Thus someone simply making up a guest bedroom can fix a problem and in discussion with the guest arrange for them to have a free dinner, say, as compensation. Such an attitude avoids much unnecessary checking and consultation, but it can also prompt change.

Why organisations must change

Any organisation must remain successful to survive. For many in the private sector that means being profitable: with investment coming from outside the organisation to fund growth and development and satisfy stakeholders such as those owning shares in the company. Non-profit organisations, ranging from charities to government departments, must also succeed in achieving their objectives, whatever they may be, and these must necessarily involve financial ones in some form.

The pressure on both kinds of organisation has never been greater. Certainly competition has broadened and intensified and, in a world where huge businesses can operate from someone's garage and trade over the internet, non-traditional competition can be as threatening as conventional competitors. More competition is international too, old borders and restrictions are disappearing and more and more operators see the world, or a major part of it, as their market. Here too the IT revolution has provided more and different methods of communicating with and servicing markets than ever before and this compounds greater competitiveness. Such trends and developments mean that change is needed more often than in the past to keep pace, and changes are often greater, more radical, and more urgent than before.

So organisations are constantly find themselves looking to make changes, particularly to:

- **find new and improved ways of operating;**
- **revise their product or service to better satisfy customers or avoid competitive threats;**
- **reduce operating costs;**
- **improve employee efficiency and productivity in every department;**

- better achieve specific objectives (for instance profitability);
- take advantage of potential changes in everything from markets to technology.

Although change can involve as wide a variety of activity as can the organisation there are two main categories of change, each a little different in nature and thus in how we need to deal with it.

Strategic change

This kind of change affects the whole direction of the organisation. It involves doing something new or different to safeguard or take forward the organisation's success, and thus may affect anything from the design, production and marketing of a product or service to the overall business philosophy. This brings to mind the old saying that while a local taxi company may develop quite widely (offering long distance courier services say), only an organisation that defines its business more broadly as 'transportation' will ever go to the moon.

Strategic change is essentially economically driven. For instance in a commercial firm success is normally measured by profit and profit is only generated in the market place. As almost every market is nothing if not dynamic, and customers seem ever more demanding and fickle, changes are regularly necessary if profit levels are to be maintained and grown. In the public sector profit may not be involved, but there is always a financial position – for instance the balance between service levels and government funding – that needs to be achieved and this too is subject to change.

Innovative change

Here the kind of change referred to is designed to improve what is currently routinely done. So this includes changes to working practices within the organisation, particularly those that improve productivity and which are concerned with how people work together or how working processes and systems affect the way they work and what is achieved as a result. Innovative change can affect any part of the organisation: design of products, levels of service, distribution, marketing tactics and techniques, pricing and more. Ultimately the intention of all such changes is to better satisfy the various stakeholders of the organisation and, in a commercial environment, to maintain and increase profitability.

In all cases certain factors are of common importance.

Changing behaviour

Whatever kind of change may be involved, strategic or innovative, they appear first and foremost to be tangible: an organisation's product undergoes change, the growth of the internet necessitates rethinking distribution, international competition creates a need to change price and much more. But no change happens automatically or in a vacuum. All have practical implications and all involve and affect people.

The nature of a particular change will affect which people or groups of people must change and in what way. Thus a change to manufacturing processes will affect shop floor staff and a change to the way things are done; customer advice being given online instead of by telephone, say, will affect a specific set of customer service staff; in both cases managers may have to change too and, of course, someone must be the initial catalyst. The integration following a company takeover or merger will affect everyone and very different ways of working may be necessary all round, as well perhaps as a reduction in staff numbers.

If people are to change then those instigating the change must understand what influences the way people behave currently and what forces motivate them to accept change and preferably to make change willingly and well. Let's consider behaviour, then in turn the motivation that can influence it.

Influences on behaviour

All sorts of things may influence the behaviour of people, but basically there are five major influences:

1. *Attitudes:* beliefs are instrumental in creating particular attitudes and people's attitudes exert an influence on every aspect of their behaviour. This is an area demanding realism: attitudes are the most difficult of all the influences to change and if change is possible then it may take time. Real understanding is necessary. For instance, if people believe that a manager is unsympathetic (and they may have some evidence for this) then any change that manager instigates is likely to be seen as unlikely to be in their interests and resistance may be an automatic reflex. It may take a good deal of explaining or action to show that a manager's motivation is being misjudged, that they do value their staff and only then can any explanation about a proposed change be given with any real chance of being listened to, accepted and acted upon. Certainly this area must be considered: if an underlying problem in accepting and supporting change lies in the prevailing attitudes of those involved then no amount of action in other areas is likely to produce results until the problem is dealt with satisfactorily.

2. *Vision:* this too is perhaps a background factor and it is also linked to attitudes. Hardly a single organisation does not have a mission statement these days (though not all are good or even clear) and such a statement is something that highlights the issue here. If people have no clear understanding of the purpose of the organisation, or indeed department, for which they work, then any change is seen as irrelevant. A 'what's it all for?' attitude prevails, changes are likely to be viewed in isolation and thus the meaning and usefulness of them is missed. Corporate vision stems from the top of course, so there is a senior

responsibility here, and if it is one that is well executed it will certainly help facilitate change. The principle here is well illustrated by the old story of the chain gang of prisoners working in a quarry. All resented the back-breaking task; the only man who worked with enthusiasm described what he did not as breaking rocks, but as 'building a cathedral'. This may be simplistic, but the point remains: a clear and attractive vision tends to make change easier to achieve, not least because it puts whatever it is in a positive context.

3. *Knowledge:* this is the easiest element to change. Taking on board new knowledge may be entirely uncontroversial and need no more than reading a memo, though more may be necessary of course, and this links to the whole area of development and training. Sometimes a small amount of additional knowledge can be instrumental in executing a significant change; for example a few extra options in a computer process may change the whole way that a process works, making it more efficient, faster or more accurate. Knowledge, or rather the need for new knowledge, tends to go hand in hand with other changes; and again computers and the learning curve that goes with any upgrade, new development or application is a good example. Additionally, if people have the relevant knowledge that will need to be drawn on after a change, then it is one less thing for them to worry about as change approaches.

4. *Skills:* the tasks most people carry out need skills to be developed to enable them to undertake the tasks effectively. This is true of a wide range of activities: computers again make a good example, but so do the skills necessary to write a good report or make a powerful presentation. It is the combination of knowledge and skills that enables people to work effectively and achieve the results with which they are targeted. Skills are easier to acquire than attitudes are to be changed, but some time and effective methodology are needed. Like knowledge, if the skills that are needed following a change are already in place then

the transition will seem easier. In addition, once acquired then skills must be kept up to date or a skill may become redundant and need to be replaced with another. We touch again on development in Chapter 6, when we examine the need for personal change.

5. *Environment:* the culture of the workplace is also an influence on people's behaviour. For instance the manager of a department must set the 'tone' as to how things are done. If people are working well together there is pressure for everyone to fit in and work similarly (a group normally hates anyone seen as a 'passenger', who does not fit in and does less than their fair share). If people are encouraged to behave, and work effectively, then results tend to reflect this. Conversely, organisations that have *a laissez-faire* attitude and tolerate poor behaviour and thus performance tend to achieve only lacklustre results; in this context avoiding making changes has a direct negative impact.

It is the combined effect of all these various influences that creates both an effective operation and a willingness and ability to accept change and make it work. Attitudes, beliefs and the way the work environment operates create the backdrop, and the tangible knowledge and skill that people bring to their tasks complete the picture. When all these influences are 'programmed for change' then change is easier and more certain to be implemented and implemented successfully. Thus even difficult or controversial changes can be made to work if everything is primed accordingly.

The second factor identified also has a bearing.

People's motivation to change

Because there is a natural tendency to resist change (at least initially) it is important that people see it as offering some personal advantage. Such an advantage can be positive – something that provides a gain to the individual – or involves avoiding a negative. Often both pain and gain are involved, though sometimes the pain is primarily in the anticipation of something unknown or in the early stages following a change. Any manager working with a team of people should see active motivation as part of their job because it makes a difference to day-to-day operations and is especially important in the face of changes. This then needs to be addressed in three ways:

1. *In the run up to change:* initially the positive side of changes as they relate to individuals must be made clear. Benefits to the individual may be minor, involving say a change to a process that makes it just a little easier or quicker to undertake, but should still be clearly spelt out. Benefits can also be in a sense once removed: for instance a change to some aspect of customer service may benefit customers in an immediate way, but more satisfied customers are easier to deal with thus benefiting individuals who have customer service tasks to perform. Even a negative change can have longer-term benefits to some individuals: a change that involves redundancy may be unpleasant, but could contribute to a more secure working environment for those remaining in post; indeed just being one of the survivors may be motivational.

2. *After change has occurred:* every aspect of change that affects people from consultation to the change itself and dealing with any hiccups that go with it demands extra of them. This should be acknowledged and, when all goes well, praised or even specifically rewarded. A change that results in different or extended responsibilities might warrant a salary increase, but any kind of reward from extra holiday allowances to an annual team conference being held in an exotic venue might be appropriate.

3. *Relating one change to another:* the success, and the contributions that made it successful, should be noted and used in future communication. If it is simply said that something needs to change then the instinctive reaction as

we have seen may be negative. But if explanation refers to a known quantity – *it can be handled rather like the way that X was changed, and that went very smoothly* – then something people have experienced is substituted for something totally unknown and, while there may still be questions, reactions are likely to be more favourable.

Exactly how motivation is undertaken is beyond our brief, though the next section summarises some main points about how it works (and I have written extensively on the subject in another book in this *Creating Success* series, *How to Motivate People*). Two overall points are worth making here:

1. There is (sadly) no magic formula guaranteed to motivate people in an instant; many methods are available and may have to be used over some time to achieve the desired result.
2. The need for motivation should be recognised and action about it must not be skimped or regarded as a chore. Motivation is important; indeed a change is far more likely to be well executed by a well-motivated group of people than those in a negative frame of mind. Spending time on it can pay dividends.

How motivation assists change

What is most important to a manager intent on ensuring that staff support change? Without meaning to negate other factors, 10 key points to successfully adopting a motivational management style may be summarised as follows:

1. Always think about the people aspects of everything.
2. Keep a list of possible motivational actions, large and small, in mind.
3. Monitor the 'motivational temperature' regularly, and especially do so ahead of any change.

4. See the process as continuous and cumulative; it should simply accelerate in a time of change.
5. Ring the changes in terms of method to maintain interest.
6. Do not be censorious about what motivates others, either positively or negatively.
7. Beware of panaceas and easy options.
8. Make sufficient time for change.
9. Evaluate what works best within your group.
10. Remember that, in part at least, there should be a 'fun' aspect to work (and that it is your job to make sure this is so).

Make motivation a habit, and make it effective, and you may be surprised by the results. The motivation for you to motivate others is in those results and, in context here, in how well a change is then executed.

What motivates people? Well, a plethora of different things. There is, as was said, no single magic formula. Creating the right motivational climate demands continuous consideration and action. Perhaps the most important thing is recognising that positive motivation does not just happen. To make it work, the theory of motivation needs to be appreciated: some aspects of work *dilute* any motivation that may exist (the dissatisfiers); other factors *enhance* it (the motivators). The trick is to work across both, using and adjusting them to create a positive balance that acts to boost performance. A good analogy is a glasshouse: the plants thrive because it can be kept at the right temperature and there are many ways to make adjustments from turning up a heater to opening a window. So too with what is sometimes referred to as the 'motivational climate' of a group of people.

Consider the range of factors involved here, though space necessitates us concentrating on just some. First, the negative factors – or demotivators – include: unfair or illogical internal policy and administration, inappropriate or unconstructive supervision, poor working conditions, salary (who would not like to earn more?), difficult interaction with peers (and people in supporting roles), lack of status, feelings of insecurity (perhaps caused by such factors as lack of clear job descriptions or targets, rather than actual job insecurity), and the many detailed elements that flow from all these. It is easy to imagine how, with change in the offing, all these factors can easily affect things negatively.

Of course, some factors exert a more powerful negative effect than others. For example, on the demotivational side, many people tend to dislike bureaucratic admin (especially if this is not a major element of their job), which is why change that is perceived as ill thought out or inadequately explained quickly causes problems.

On the positive side people are classically motivated by achievement, recognition (of their achievements), the work itself, advancement and growth. Many jobs have some inherently motivational aspects, provided people are well chosen (good selection is also vital) and like their work. Jobs that typically demand considerable responsibility – a key motivational factor – and the ability to act alone and make decisions, are likely to appeal to staff most. It follows that getting people actively involved in a way that allows them to have an input and gives them a sense of achievement, provides a sound basis for successful change.

So, overall motivational action must be:

- *Well judged* – **the right action, at the right time (and thus at the right moment as any change is occurring), carried out in an appropriate way.**
- *Creative* – **finding new and different things to do as well as utilising tried and tested methods.**
- *Balanced* – **using a mixture of methods all well matched to the individuals involved.**
- *Continuous* – **motivation must be an inherent, ongoing part of any manager's job, not a 'when there is time' thing (though the general level may need to be cranked up in times of change).**

Finally, remember that the little things are as important as the large. Incentive payments may be powerful motivators, but so is saying 'Well done!' Let's give the final word to Mary Kay Ash, a successful American businesswoman, who said: 'If you think you can, you can and if you think you can't, you're right.' This is worth keeping in mind. If people do not believe a satisfactory change is possible, or that they cannot cope with their part in it, then it can be doomed before it begins. The manager who motivates gives themselves, and their people, an edge – an edge that in times of change can make all the difference between success and failure.

The moral here is clear: in any organisation that seeks to make changes, especially if this must be done on a regular basis, managers should address motivation issues on a regular basis. Some stem from specific moments and processes, like the link between job appraisal and the subsequent development of skills. Others are ongoing issues that need to be constantly borne in mind. In a hectic work place it is easy for action here to be skimped: how many managers can honestly say that they have said 'Well done!' sufficiently often in the past month? (Can you?) Yet managers who are on top of these things will always find they have created a situation in which it is easier to instigate change and do so without undue hassle.

Action

The nature of change is such that it encompasses a wide range of circumstances from large corporate changes to small (though significant) personal ones. The lesson here is clear: awareness of change – likely or actual – is paramount across much of what you do and must be accommodated in your thinking about what you do and how you do it.

We now turn, in the next chapter, to the topic of preparatory action.

2

Preparing for change

In this chapter a variety of issues that must be considered in the run up to change are set out ahead of reviewing the implementation stage. The different aspects involved overlap and together make clear why people talk of 'change management'. There is a process involved here and the various matters that affect its likely success must be dealt with systematically; and this all starts in the preparatory stage. The danger is poor results if preparation is delayed or skimped; time spent up front pays dividends.

Any change should prompt positive benefits and in many cases these need to be long lasting. Preparation should make a positive outcome more likely. It should also smooth the process, ensuring that the fact of change does not cause disruption of operations or upset to people (who may then perform less well). Essentially change aims to move people to a new way of thinking and operating and does so in a manner that is compatible with the structure of an organisation, its strategy and the processes and systems that are currently in train.

Because any organisation is nothing without its people, making changes demands taking the people with you. Unless everyone, at every level, understands the change and is committed to it and motivated to want to make it work then it will fail, or at the very least be diluted in its effect. Similarly if changes are in conflict in some way with existing culture or processes then they will be more difficult to implement in a straightforward manner.

Barriers to change

If change is to be made successfully then it must be prepared for realistically in a way that takes into account the things that may make it difficult. Of course, difficulties can be many and varied. For example I once saw a major change held up only by one key player because the date of implementation clashed with a special holiday they were planning, though this was not voiced up front. But the main areas that cause problems are:

- **employee resistance (often prejudiced and/or ill-informed);**
- **culture disruption (which can increase people's resistance);**
- **lack of agreement and vision (especially at senior/strategic level);**
- **ineffective planning;**
- **poor, confusing communication;**
- **lack of appropriate skills (especially if new skills will be necessary in changed situations);**
- **current pressure, which can all too easily mean changes that should be made are delayed or rushed through on an ill-considered basis that causes problems.**

People and cultural factors predominate here and everything mentioned suggests the need to consider how things will work in advance and think things through in terms of the broad picture and the long term-implications. It should be borne in mind that many changes seem to go well initially, but problems appear down the line because things have not been thought through. As many companies began to create websites in the early days of the IT revolution it was common for the job of keeping the site up to date to be underestimated in terms of both cost, time and specialised skills.

Barriers are inherent, but once identified they must be addressed, that is removed, reduced or worked around.

The success factors

While care is assuredly necessary, it is not right to labour the difficulties of change. Changes are made, and made successfully, in organisations around the world every day; albeit when their doing so looks straightforward it is because someone is planning carefully to make it so. The factors that tend to influence success most, and thus need most attention in preparation, spell out, in the way much beloved of trainers, the word SUCCESS. When everything is well in all of these areas then the chances of success are maximised. The letters stand for:

- *Shared vision:* **there needs to be a clear, positive statement describing where the change is taking you and why and this must be understood and appreciated by all.**
- *Understanding of the organisation:* **sound analysis of the organisation is necessary to ensure that the identification of salient factors is done, especially anything that will need special attention.**
- *Culture compatibility:* **any change must be implemented bearing in mind the nature of the organisation and how it works so that change can be made to fit the current style and methodology.**
- *Clear communication:* **this is essential throughout the process (further details are described in Chapter 4).**
- *Expert assistance:* **the way change is undertaken must be that which is most likely to create success and if that needs some outside assistance then so be it.**

- _Strong leadership:_ change goes better with a sponsor (someone sometimes referred to as a champion): this is someone at a senior level (or with suitable influence) who is manifestly, even enthusiastically, in favour and makes their views known (however much they may or may not be involved in the actual process).
- _Stakeholder commitment:_ when it is said that everyone must be involved what this means must be worked out carefully in terms of who needs to be included; for instance, employees, management, shareholders, external people such as government, customers and suppliers – and more.

Three overall factors predominate here: people, organisation and corporate culture

People factors

Clearly people must be considered. Their acceptance and support is necessary to success. People are individuals. They will react differently – depending on their character, circumstances and position in the organisation – and their reactions can sometimes be difficult to forecast. For instance, people's reaction will vary in terms of the personal and corporate view they take of something. One might expect more senior people to take a more corporate view of things, but this may not always be the case.

Everybody involved needs to be considered by those instigating change, and that means both those seemingly supportive as well as those where the likelihood of resistance is strong. In considering people it is worth both anticipating some resistance and trying to ascertain just why and how any resistance might be expressed. Such may include people:

- **Not seeing the point of change: which may mean they do not understand or simply prefer things the way they are despite a rational argument.**

- Being busy: and either not giving the matter the attention which would allow it to be explained or feeling it constitutes 'the last straw'.
- Feeling threatened: directly or indirectly and in major or minor ways, from losing their job to losing a perk – such a threat can be real, imagined or real but overrated.
- Anticipating cultural problems: for instance seeing their team or support system changing.
- Simply being against change on principle (and not just older people) or, in some instances, resisting as a gesture in the 'war between them and us'.

Tip
The question of *how* resistance might show itself is important: this can range from rumours and rumblings that do little real damage to orchestrated attempts to derail plans, perhaps by a formal group like a union. Different manifestations of discontent will need different tactics planning to combat them.

Negative responses can be almost like grieving: that is mourning the status quo which is safe, familiar and non-threatening. This kind of reaction goes through several stages:

1. *Immobilisation:* a stage when people simply ignore what is going on, doing so on an 'out of sight, out of mind' basis.
2. *Denial:* then people begin to resist, their response becomes more active and can link to the third stage.
3. *Anger:* if denial turns to anger then responses become more active and more disruptive (and are often ill thought out).

4. *Negotiation:* anger, especially if it gets them nowhere, can then turn to attempts to alter the change, perhaps diluting its effect (for example, requesting a trial period first rather than a full, permanent change).

5. *Depression:* if negotiation fails then people are apt to go into their shells again – a stage where there will be little active collaboration.

6. *Testing:* finally, if the inevitable is recognised or if explanations finally get through, people reluctantly try the new ways.

7. *Acceptance:* if the change is well judged then, while there may still be some (personal) downsides, people find that it is sensible and accept it for the future.

Clearly recognising where people are amongst these seven stages is useful in pushing things forward. If people are in favour and initial reactions are favourable, this too may go through five stages (which might be visualised as a classic bell-shaped curve with initial pessimism first rising and then moving to acceptance and compliance):

1. *Uninformed optimism:* at this stage people react positively at least to the extent of being confident that a change will be good.

2. *Informed pessimism:* as information is provided and understanding begins realism takes over from bald confidence and this can raise negative issues.

3. *Realism:* as understanding is completed any lingering pessimism is replaced by confidence.

4. *Informed optimism:* then as the process of change moves on information and understanding finally prompt full optimism – this will be okay – and involvement is engaged.

5. *Acceptance and support:* finally full support and cooperation is the order of the day.

This transition may take a while, the time varying depending on the nature of the change and, of course, how it is handled;

equally it may be almost instant for straightforward change. Understanding people's likely reaction and following their actual one is the first step to moving them more rapidly and easily to acceptance. For instance, if it is recognised that people are sticking, failing to move from stage 3 to 4 (in which cooperative action begins), then additional or revised communication may push matters on.

Organisation factors

The organisation itself is also instrumental in influencing how easy it is to change. First, the nature and purpose of the organisation is relevant. In some fields, perhaps IT is a broad example, change is an accepted part of normal operations; certainly it is said that if your computer works well, it must be obsolete! A new model seems to come out before you have an initial one run in and operating as you want. In such an environment change should be well accepted, but even in this case there can be problems if change goes beyond what people are well used to or if it is seen to be more personal in effect.

Secondly, other factors about the nature of the organisation contribute. As change means changing people's behaviour, it is how the organisation affects people and conditions their attitudes that is crucial. For instance in a flatter organisation structure, one where the hierarchy has few layers, it may be inherently easier to find senior champions for change as the senior people are not out of reach. Sheer size is a factor too, more people, more locations, more management layers and everything from consultation to communication is likely to be more complex and take longer too.

Certainly some thought about how ready the organisation, or part if not all of it, is to adopt and work with change is sensible and useful. One measure that is now common (and was originated in the work of Harvey and Brown, change management authors) categorises readiness for change into four levels, arrived at by comparing two factors – stability of the environment and management adaptability – each high and low in a matrix.

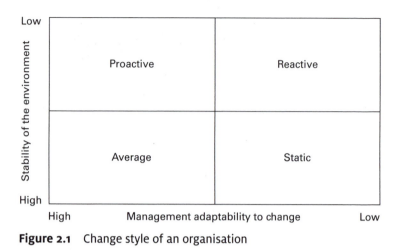

Figure 2.1 Change style of an organisation

The four types thus described are then defined:

1. *Proactive:* because of the dynamic environment in which they operate, in these organisations change is the norm; management, including top management, promote a vision of action to keep ahead of the game and change is seen as an inherent part of that.
2. *Reactive:* such organisations change only when they have to, and sometimes they react to environmental factors (such as competitive threats) only grudgingly and with change being imperfectly executed.
3. *Average:* most organisations are like this. They do change and they do keep up, but change causes some difficulty and is sometimes late and poor in execution.
4. *Static:* common in organisations with a rigid hierarchy and a fixed style of management, the need for change can cause difficulties here and it is difficult to get acceptance for it.

Clearly there is merit in an organisation acting to ensure that it is open to change and of moving actively towards that if necessary. In the meantime it pays to recognise how any difficulties will manifest themselves. You need to allow for them, or indeed to build on the strengths of a group used to change and able to adapt quickly.

For an individual designated to head up change programmes, the 'good change' organisation will promote feelings likely to assist the process. Such a 'change agent' will:

- **be motivated to be involved and in charge of change;**
- **feel they have appropriate responsibility and authority to effect the change (or seek and secure it);**
- **be confident of the hierarchy around them, knowing who they report to and who they can call on for assistance;**
- **have been well briefed, and if required trained in any specific skills necessary for what must be done.**

Thus those designating someone to head up a change programme must make sure that they are well equipped and confident to run it, and if they are seconded to this it must be made clear that this is a vote of confidence and that they are regarded as well able to cope. That said, if anyone seconded to a change role should have reservations, gaps in their knowledge or skills or concerns about what support may be available they should raise it up front. There is no merit in trying to wing it and then foundering half way through a project; executing change is difficult enough without embarking on it poorly briefed or with an inadequate armoury.

Corporate culture factors

The nature of the organisation is characterised by the culture it embraces – how it works. A prevailing corporate culture consists of:

- **the various ways in which operations work in an organisation, or a part of it (departments or divisions can vary);**
- **practices that are normal, acceptable or unacceptable;**
- **formal rules of operation and the second layer of norms that usually underpin them.**

Everything combines to make organisations very different culturally and the options are many and wide. Retail chain Marks & Spencer does not run its operations like a bank, nor Holiday Inn like budget airline Ryanair. What makes each individual organisation, well, individual, stems from a number of factors, and these include:

- **The prevailing management style: this can vary enormously from dictatorial to heavily consultative. Vision and forward thinking are an important part of this in terms of promoting change.**
- **History: a long-established organisation can reflect lessons hard learnt which can affect current operations; a newly established organisation is likely to be different.**
- **Ownership: a family business is different to one with shareholders to be satisfied and ownership that is distant, dictatorial or both will certainly affect an organisation's ability to change easily.**
- **Purpose: different missions – profit, charity, growth, quality and so on – tend to foster different styles and thus different cultures.**
- **Scale of operations: whether operations reflect a global presence or a small-scale local one will clearly have a bearing.**

The above are prime but other factors can be added. An organisation's facility with IT is a factor; so too is the kind of people employed (their level of qualification, skill and proficiency). All this certainly results in there being outward signs that indicate the kind of culture at work. Such signs include:

- **style of premises (location, type, decoration and design);**
- **staff attitudes (customer service can measure this);**
- **working habits (hours worked for instance);**
- **appearance and conduct of people (even in less formal times people must normally be smart and always customer focused and efficient).**

Such things can be powerful in their influence. For example, smart offices no doubt make everyone feel good; ones with an even stronger element of design and grandeur may impress both staff (perhaps boosting their confidence – *we must be good!*) and customers alike. However, go too far and the message becomes one of arrogance and can be off putting. I once saw this quote – 'never do business with a company which has a fountain in reception' – the implication being that such self-aggrandisment means that it is unlikely to deliver value for money.

The precise nature of the culture within an organisation can affect how change is handled within it. While everyone is different, there are four overall cultural types:

1. *Centralised power culture:* in many organisations, especially well-established entrepreneurial ones, power and decision making tends to be centralised, that is heavily influenced by a small number of people at senior level. In such organisations decisions may be easy to get, though they may be primarily based on a combination of experience and hunch (and so may not always be the best as they will often involve little consultation). Nevertheless to prompt change it is especially important that such senior people are involved and give their support to whatever must be done.

2. *Functional culture:* in this type of organisation communication is good within functions and up and down the organisation, but is poor across functional boundaries. Faced with change, achieving accord can be time consuming and effort must be well placed to follow current practice and yet get messages around the organisation. Again senior commitment helps.

3. *Task-based culture:* here the predominant factor in the way the organisation works is the project or task. Communication is flexible and there is little rigid hierarchy; in terms of change it means that many people at all levels may need to be involved and that while communicating with them is easy efforts must be made to include everyone necessary despite the low incidence of a formal structure.

4. *Individual focused culture:* this is typical in service companies, where professional staff members pursue their own projects and interests and yet must link to organisational goals as well. This is the least common of the four types, and organising to involve everyone in such a disparate situation needs care and effort.

As you plan to instigate change, it does help to make the process easier if you are clear just how your organisation works. You need to know what the so-called 'levers' are, where and how influence can be brought to bear – what buttons to press as it were.

Careful, systematic preparation which is given sufficient time is something that will assist many activities; its positive influence is very obvious when it is absent. This is rather like the situation when someone stands up to make an important presentation and has not given preparation its due. It is also something that experience shows it is all too easy to skimp on in the heat of the moment as many of the prevailing pressures demand action 'now'.

As change is rarely easy, it is worth making some resolutions about your commitment to preparation and remembering that ill-considered initiation of change is likely to be downright difficult.

Preparation smoothes the way and what is done also acts to guide things along as matters progress. Ultimately a checklist is needed – a classic action plan that specifies:

- **what will be done;**
- **who is responsible (for both initiating matters and the tasks necessary along the way);**
- **when things will be done (all aspects of timing, sensibly including some contingency).**

The actions can vary enormously and many, as we will see in Chapter 4, concern that which communicating change involves. In the next chapter we look at the practicalities of making change successful and the sequence of events that it necessitates.

Action

It should be no surprise that, as with so many things that must be done in corporate life, preparation is important. A great deal can be at stake with even small changes in the offing, so regarding preparation – thorough preparation – as a prerequisite is only sensible. In a busy life it can seem a chore and get skimped; that is a mistake. Take time to be ready for change – it increases the chances of success in every aspect of its implementation.

Prompting successful change

Preparation is very important, as we have seen in the last chapter: it means thinking everything through, anticipating problems and objections and adopting a considered and systematic approach, and it is this that we consider next.

Factors facilitating change

Let me say again, for the most part, change does not just happen; certainly well ordered change does not. It needs to be prompted and an active approach to initiating it is necessary. What conditions need to be satisfied if change is going to be successfully made? Several things are important and these apply to one degree or another, whatever the scale and nature of the change is and whether it will affect an individual, a small group, a department or the whole organisation. These main factors are as follows.

1. Clear purpose

It is axiomatic that change is hardly likely to be made successfully on an ad hoc basis. There needs to be a defined purpose behind it, indeed this should direct it. This in turn means that change must:

- **relate to overall organisational goals;**
- **be well defined;**
- **have the desired outcomes clearly specified.**

Let's say a few words about each of these points before going further. The change should:

- *Relate to overall organisational goals:* **the reason for making any change must link to measurement. This may be personal: management on a profit-sharing incentive will be motivated to make changes that increase profit and in such circumstances it is always much better to say that profits must be lifted by 10 per cent or whatever rather than some vague statement such as aiming to increase 'as much as possible' (this tends to be a self-fulfilling prophesy, however small the increase actually proves to be). Whatever the mission of the organisation and whatever senior officers of the company are motivated to do, a change will stand the best chance of speedy implementation if it is tightly bound to this.**
- *Be well defined:* **changes can be positive or negative in the sense that they may be designed to take advantage of an opportunity or to combat a difficulty; in either case they will only go well if they are clearly defined and have clear objectives. Whatever is necessary must be done at this stage: consideration, consultation, assessment and reassessment – but no further action should be taken until it is clear what the intention is. At the core of this is setting objectives. (The box opposite sets out some guidelines.)**

- *The desired outcomes of the change should be specified:* this too links to objective setting. It is axiomatic that a change requires something to be different after it is made. This ties in to the stages of objective setting (see box) designed to stop it being vague. You need to describe what will come from the change and, what is more, describe it in a way that those people affected by it, and whose support you need to make it work, can visualise it. It is useless to say only that things will be 'better' or that a process will be 'more efficient'; the specifics must be spelt out. It can help here to identify a benchmark: for example as part of the description to say that things need to change so that it (the organisation, department or whatever) is like (something else with which people are familiar).

It may be obvious, but it is sufficiently important to state: in part all of this is for the instigator of change to bear in mind. Someone intent on change may feel they are clear what they want to do and achieve, but the thinking that defining the situation and setting objectives demands is invaluable in clarifying intentions, identifying things overlooked and stating clearly exactly what will be done and why. That done change can be embarked upon with confidence.

Setting objectives

A statement like *my objective is to improve customer service* is not much help unless you have set out some clear actions and specified steps to be taken along the way. It is said that objectives should be SMART. This well-known mnemonic stands for:

- *Specific* – objectives should be expressed clearly and precisely.

- *Measurable* – it must be possible to tell if you have achieved your objectives after the change is made (for example, the difference between saying you want to 'improve customer service' or 'halve response times to telephone enquires' or, better still, 'ensure all telephones in customer services are answered within three rings' allows measurement).
- *Achievable* – what is to be changed must not be so difficult as to be unachievable, otherwise the plan that goes with it similarly becomes invalid and of no practical help in gaining support or taking things forward; though this should *not*, of course, be taken to mean you should avoid aiming high.
- *Realistic* – objectives must fit with an analysis of what you want and with your broad intentions; it might technically be a valid objective to aim for something possible but not ideal (a new product might be possible to develop and launch, but if it did not fit the range, or fitted too closely so that it would lead to a decrease in sales on existing lines, then further development might make sense first). Unrealistic objectives will not be helpful; indeed if achieved they can do more harm than good.
- *Timed* – this is important; objectives are not to be achieved 'eventually', 'soon' or 'in due course' but by a particular moment: when do you aim to do something, at then end of this year, end of next year or when?

The factors here both direct objective setting and provide a checklist enabling you to verify that any objectives you have set for change do make sense and will inform the process to come, helping it to succeed.

There may be no need for elaborate documentation here. On a small scale any objectives and any plans may be purely for your own guidance, but a few notes on paper may be useful and there are times (when major change is afoot and many people will be involved) when your initial thoughts need formalising into a plan, report or proposal and the details clearly stipulated. If you not only know which road you should be on, but have taken steps to make sure you go purposively along it, then that is a good start as you contemplate any change.

Every (significant) change initiative needs someone to support and actively lead the process. This role may be combined with the hands-on one of actually project managing the change and attending to the details. But it may not and thus it is useful to consider the role of leading change in isolation before going further. Leadership is the second factor facilitating change.

2. Defining the leadership of change

Leadership can be defined as inspiring people to do (willingly) what is required; in this context to make the changes that are necessary, promptly and effectively in a way that links to results. This in turn means ensuring that people are confident that things will be improved by the change and can see clearly the route that needs to be taken to get to the better future. Whoever does this, and perhaps the first job here is to make sure it is not a role that is falling between the cracks, they must be correctly positioned. If a change is to be organisation wide then the leader must be at, or close to, the top. If it is more local then the appropriate level of manager needs to be involved.

That said change leadership must:

- **relate clearly and accurately to the objectives set;**
- **orchestrate the needs, wants and feeling of the people it aims to lead towards those goals.**

In turn, this style of change leadership must relate to both the level of perceptions and behaviour and to the actual methods and 'mechanics' of putting the change in place. So with an eye on the behavioural side of things the leader should:

1. Exercise professionalism and clout to ensure they are seen as the leader.
2. Respect and empathise with the people who are affected by the change (and be seen to do so).
3. Communicate clearly and prompt trust through genuine consultation.
4. Recognise and use the experience, knowledge and skill of others.
5. Remain visibly involved throughout the process.
6. Be easily accessible: to answer questions and confer in any way necessary. Your availability must be genuine: too many managers say that their door is always open and are then never behind it.

Note: the note in point 2 – to be 'seen to be doing so' – really applies throughout this section. Leadership cannot be exercised from the shadows.

As the actual project progresses the leader should:

1. Ensure it fits with the overall corporate vision for the longer term future.
2. Define and communicate clear and specific objectives.
3. Put in place any controls necessary to monitor progress.
4. Consult as necessary before finalising what will be done and how.
5. Set out clearly the methodology and timing and specify the roles and tasks of everyone involved.
6. Manage and monitor the process along the way to ensure all goes well.
7. Communicate clearly and regularly throughout the duration of the project.

8. Provide feedback afterwards about how things have gone (all being well this should consist of motivational messages praising how people have ensured matters concluded successfully; though any lessons learnt may need flagging too).

All this adds up to a not inconsiderable task. The leader's role is vital. On some scales one manager, you perhaps, combines the role of leader and project – change – manager. Alternatively there may be a whole team of people involved in implementation and change may run across hierarchies and functions.

3. The people factor

Here three issues are important.

1. *Behavioural considerations:* aspects of people's behaviour when faced with change have been commented on earlier in the text and particularly in the last chapter. Essentially two factors must be accommodated. First, likely reactions: what they are likely to be and why and what should be done to get people on side? Secondly, attendant changes that may be necessary to make things work. For example, if it is necessary to improve productivity and cut costs then this may mean redundancies. Additional changes alongside the new work practices of those remaining may increase acceptability (an example of this might be new incentive payments).
2. *Involvement:* it has been said that understanding of planned change must be rapidly followed by support and cooperation. This means involving people, and perhaps giving them ownership of the change: ownership means that they do not just support it but begin to think of it as 'our idea' and thus will implement it with more enthusiasm. Different stakeholders may need approaching in different ways and each must be hooked by something that is truly relevant to *them*.

3. *Briefing:* beyond this anyone – everyone – who has a role to play needs a thorough briefing both about what will happen and, if appropriate, what they need to do. This means significant, systematic and careful communication (the subject of the next chapter) put over in an appropriate fashion; everyone has heard horror stories of the reverse, people fired by text messages, say.

4. Selecting the methodology

Any change is, in a sense, a project and large-scale ones need project managing. The two different kinds of change identified earlier need different approaches.

1. *Innovative changes:* here changes are related to ongoing processes so there is, or can be – or indeed should be – regular ongoing processes in place to identify the need for change and set things in train. By this I mean such techniques as TQM (total quality management) designed to improve performance while linking positively to customer satisfaction – see the box opposite. Other changes are instigated on a one-off basis and may involve any method that fits the area of operation in which they sit.
2. *Strategic changes:* these are by definition more likely to be one-off in nature, and they may be more all-embracing and substantial than innovative changes. Different types of strategic change demand different approaches. First there is *management change* – that is changing the way the organisation, or part of it, is managed or structured in terms of organisation, hierarchy and roles and responsibilities. That said it is possible that some changes here have both innovative and strategic scope. Secondly there are *procedural changes*. These affect the way things are organised and done and involve everything from standards to information systems and processes. There are clearly a plethora of

ways of handling systems and processes and thus many opportunities to change them. As an example, I sent an email recently to King of Shaves. I had an email back within hours, a prepaid envelope arrive the following morning to return something to them and the whole process was easy and professional. Conversely we all have horror stories illustrating that such systems can be the very reverse of this, some involving weeks of frustration. Thirdly, a large and ongoing area of change, *technical change*. This can involve different ways of doing things – classically computerisation – but may also focus on a range of operational factors from organising production (such an area presents many options for change right through to moving production completely to a low-cost country) to identifying and exploiting new markets.

Total quality management (TQM)

This term was coined to formalise various ideas linked to continuous improvement and drew on the original ideas of *kaizen* (see pages 10). TQM seeks to ensure commitment to ongoing improvement (initially in production processes though the concept is now more widely applied) by setting clear objectives and monitoring progress towards them. It assumes that changing things necessitates changing people and their attitudes and gives a clear priority to quality so that things are got right first time and consistency becomes a constant watchword. Here changes are based on well-identified need (for instance of customers whether internal or external) and the process is actively led in a way that aims to get people working together and remove friction. Ensuring that people are able to do all this at every level is part of the process and thus there is a link to training and development.

TQM is not a rigid process. Many organisations use the idea and do so in a variety of forms and under a variety of names (for example, Total Involvement, Customers First, Focus on Customers, Working Together and more). It is a proven approach, though one that needs ongoing commitment and effort to maintain. In today's competitive markets it can achieve much to maintain organisational success.

Making it work

Whilst every individual change needs individually approaching, it is useful to start with a common framework: that is a sequence of stages that will carry you through most programmes of change. Such a sequence may provide a sensible approach even to simple areas of change, one needing little consideration or time. More often things are more complicated and going through carefully in this kind of way is more of a necessity. The main stages are set out below and then a more detailed picture described for both innovative and strategic change.

1. *Analysis:* investigating what needs changing, why and whether the organisation is ready for it.
2. *Designing the change:* fitting what will be done to the circumstances and the people.
3. *Planning:* setting out the detailed approach and methodology.
4. *Communications:* specifying when, how and to whom the change must be communicated.
5. *Selecting the people:* who will be involved in any way in implementation.
6. *Obtaining senior support:* what is often called a champion of change.
7. *Consultation:* something that may well need to predate the rest of the process (or be part of the analysis) and continue in various ways throughout.

Implementation of innovative changes

Innovative changes are those to practices and processes that can be regarded to some extent as routine; certainly in most organisations a great many such changes are usually necessary to keep operations at peak efficiency. A typical sequence might be as shown in Figure 3.1.

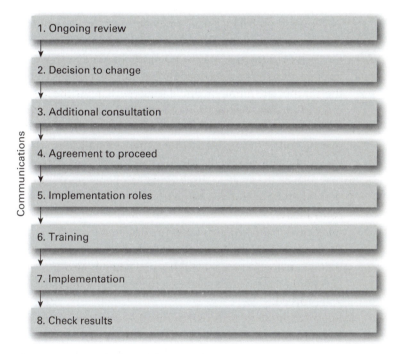

Figure 3.1   A typical sequence for innovative change

Some detail on each of these stages follows:

1. *Ongoing review:* most, but certainly not all, such changes will come from various ongoing processes of review

and consultation. Such include schemes such as quality circles and more routine departmental meetings, which should have an eye on change as well as acting to review short-term operations and performance. From such deliberations ideas occur to make positive changes that will affect performance in a variety of ways: efficiency, effectiveness, cost-effectiveness, product performance, profitability and more.

2. *Decision to change:* this is the point at which a specific decision is made to go beyond the idea stage and investigate or implement something. This can be made at a variety of levels, but is probably typically at department head or middle management level. The decision may need documenting: that is recording (this may be no more than the minutes of a departmental meeting or could be more formal) and, at the appropriate moment, circulating (perhaps as the first stage of further consultation or explanation).

3. *Additional consultation:* with matters agreed in principle it may be politic to consult further either generally or with those who will be specifically involved or affected. This may also be the stage to think about any benchmarking that might be useful as a comparison as the change process continues.

4. *Agreement to proceed:* this takes the decision to act to the next stage. Here the methods to be used are agreed, that is the how, and what will happen when is also specified to ensure it is clear exactly how implementation will proceed.

5. *Implementation roles:* as part of the plan developed in point 4 specifics need to be added in terms of *who* will do what and when. Then people involved will need briefing – jointly or separately – so that they are clear on what their roles entail.

6. *Training:* this stage is not always necessary, but should be part of the overall assessment: if new knowledge or skills are going to be needed they should ideally be

developed ahead of going further. Certainly training should be considered as it is not uncommon for a change to be made, a potentially good one too, and then for it to founder in some way because training has not been implemented.

7. *Implementation:* here the various actions are project managed though the list of things to be done clearly varies depending on what change is being made.

8. *Check results:* this should be built into the plan from the beginning, specifying who will do it and when. Any lessons learned should be fed back into the ongoing review process (the first point in this list).

Alongside this list is one more stage, added here as it runs in parallel with the sequence above: and that is *communications.* The importance of this is made abundantly clear through the text; indeed this is given its own chapter.

Note: the complexity here in planning or timetabling terms is obvious. It makes sense to highlight the key steps in writing and in checklist form. This can be done in two ways: either listing the actions chronologically; or listing each stage as a group of actions (again in chronological order).

The choice here is personal, based on what seems most straightforward to you and is most manageable. A suggestion for this checklist is shown in Figures 3.2 and 3.3.

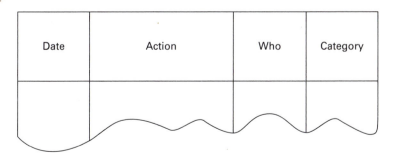

Date	Action	Who	Category

Figure 3.2 Action checklist (1)

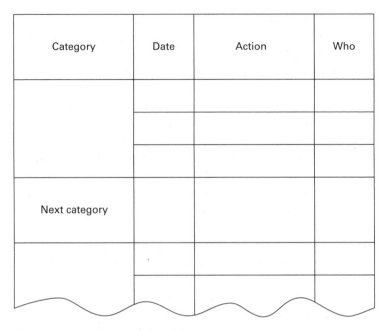

Category	Date	Action	Who
Next category			

Figure 3.3 Action checklist (2)

Implementation of strategic change

Strategic changes, those affecting longer term, broader and more radical matters, demand some differences (see Figure 3.4).

Again each of these stages is commented on in turn:

1. *Ongoing management/planning:* at senior level, certainly at board level, and in conjunction with the ongoing cycle of business (and marketing), planning matters of strategic change will arise; indeed it may be a specific intention that they do.
2. *Specific consultation:* an idea may immediately need investigating, refining or confirming by others within the

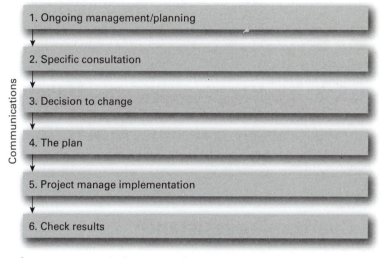

Figure 3.4   A typical sequence for strategic change

organisation who are more immediately involved so that its necessity and practicality are verified.

3. *Decision to change:* following stage 2 a formal decision may need to be made to move ahead (one that may well need to allocate funding and thus may need to follow some costing). This stage confirms the senior support necessary and also needs to brief and involve others who will be involved in seeing the change through.

4. *The plan:* the how, when and who aspects need timetabling (as for innovative changes) and wider communication may start in earnest here too.

5. *Project management/implementation:* here the actual work of implementation starts; in terms of a strategic change this may be both substantial and take place over a significant span of time.

6. *Check results:* again monitoring should be built into the process and feedback should be arranged so that it can inform future decisions.

Again it should be noted that *communication* is essential to success and must range through, and alongside, the process as necessary. You can link what is said here to Figures 3.1 and 3.2, to have in mind a manageable way of planning the detail and tracking and managing progress.

However systematic and well organised the process of implementing change may be, it is important to instil a positive approach to it but because resistance to change is so common, overcoming that is a prime skill of communication for any change agent.

Overcoming resistance

There are some changes that are instantly welcomed, sometimes even in a long-anticipated way – *at last, thank goodness.* But this is by no means always the case and resistance may well be a natural reaction, whether ultimately justified or not. For instance, people often vote for the status quo and keeping things as they are, just for the sake of familiarity. But the job is to carry people with you through the process, moving them through three states:

1. *Defiance:* initially people are often simply against the change and express this either openly or in a covert manner.
2. *Compliance:* at this stage people adopt a grudging acceptance; they go along with the change, but a lack of enthusiasm may slow progress and some active action against it can persist.
3. *Agreement:* now, careful persuasion having worked perhaps, there is cooperation: a change is being organised and people are involved – working with the instigators to actively see it happen and make it successful.

Only when the third stage is reached is change likely to be made successfully in a way that works and which keeps working.

Achieving the transition from one stage to another is assisted primarily by the nature and style of communication used during the run up to change (and this is reviewed in Chapter 6), though ill-considered change that everyone can see is bad may not be saved by any kind of communication. In context here we focus on the active techniques of overcoming resistance.

First, bear in mind one overall factor about agreement, because most often people do not make snap judgements. Instinctive resistance to change is a snap judgement, but it is one based only on assumption and perhaps prejudice. People normally weigh things up before agreeing and like to feel they are making an informed decision. An analogy helps illustrate this: see the box below.

Deciding to agree

Agreeing to go along with or better still support a change requires a decision to be made. How exactly do people make decisions? They:

- **consider the options;**
- **consider the advantages and disadvantages of each;**
- **weigh up the overall way in which they compare;**
- **select what seems to be, on balance, the best course of action to take.**

This does not mean that the option of change must have no downsides; realistically this may simply not be possible. It means assessing things and deciding something presents an acceptable option, one where the pluses outweigh the minuses. The analogy of a balance or weighing scales is a good one to keep in mind. Imagine a set of old-fashioned scales with a container on each side. One contains a variety of plus signs, the other minuses. The signs are of different sizes because some elements of the argument are more important than others – they weigh more heavily on the scales. Additionally, some signs represent tangible matters. Others are more subjective – and some, for instance assessing where you will work following an office relocation – have both tangible and intangible aspects to them. Both can be a powerful component of any case and help people decide what to think about a change.

A final point completes the picture here: some decisions are more important than others and therefore may be seen to warrant more thought. Where a decision is of this sort people may actively want it to be *considered.* They want to feel that the process of making it has been sensible and thorough (and therefore their decision is more likely to be a good one); and they may want other people (their manager, say) to feel the same. In either case, this feeling may lengthen the process of persuading them.

The moral from the box above is that overcoming resistance means persuading people that the balance they are forming a picture of in their minds is a positive one; overcoming resistance means dealing with the minuses (and perhaps also enhancing the pluses).

However, before any point of resistance is addressed it should be considered and regarded as a source of feedback. There is after all a chance that if a significant number of people do not think a change is a good idea, then they may be right: perhaps it's *not* a good idea. So some objective review (or re-review) may be necessary and possibly some fine tuning too.

If the change is right and must be made to go well, then resistance must be changed to support it. But first consider whether resistance can be avoided through anticipation.

Anticipating possible resistance

You will know from experience that objections are not just possible, they are likely – indeed many say that receiving none is a sign of a total lack of interest. And if people are simply not engaged then they are unlikely to give the support you may well need. As your experience with this sort of thing grows few objections should come as a complete surprise to you. You come to know the sort of thing that gets raised. Further you learn the kind of things different types of people raise – the ones who are obsessed with every last tiny detail, the ones who are suspicious of any management promise, and more.

So to some extent you can, as you prepare to initiate change, anticipate what may be asked, and be ready to deal with it effectively. Of course, sometimes something will come out of the blue, and always the objection may be put in a different way from how it has occurred in the past. Preparing for objections does not mean you can stop thinking during the process to come or that you always have a 'pat' answer ready, but it will make dealing with resistance more certain and make it less likely that it will unbalance the case you present so that staff or others reject it. Some objections you may be able to prevent arising at all by thinking ahead. Prevention may be used as effectively as cure in this area.

A further consideration is that there may be objections that remain unspoken. This does not mean they are not in people's minds: some will be and will form part of the balance upon which they will ultimately decide to accept the change or not. Where experience shows that this is likely to be happening it may be necessary for you to raise the issue yourself, perhaps early on or during the consultation stage, in order to deal with it and get a point out of the frame. This is best approached head on. In a meeting you might say: *You have been wondering about XYZ I'm sure – let me spend a minute explaining how we deal with that. You have not mentioned ABC: do you have any questions about that?*

And if you have thought through the answer, or at least the kind of answer necessary, then you can deal with the matter and perhaps also make it seem reasonably inconsequential.

Providing an answer

Never attempt to deal with an objection until you have sufficient information. If you assume wrongly exactly what is meant or treat a serious point superficially you will quickly be in trouble and make matters worse. Resistance must not be allowed to put you on the defensive. What is called 'sparring' helps set the scene. Thus any acknowledgement should be positive and in a meeting can usefully give you a moment to think. Thus if something is raised, perhaps a sceptical comment about timing, saying something like *That's a good point, timing is key here, let me explain in more detail how we aim to deal with this...* ahead of any comment makes it clear that you are thinking about the point and treating it seriously. You will find that another useful device is to respond unashamedly to a question by asking another question. This will be understood and accepted; after all how can you be expected to comment sensibly about a point until you know exactly what lies behind it? More than one question may be quite acceptable, though you should make it clear what you are doing: *That's a fair point, let me make sure I understand exactly what you mean, can you tell me ...* This is an important point as simple questions or comments may either disguise a deeper point or, more often, can have many interpretations. Consider an example. If someone comments on cost – always important – saying something like: *That is very expensive*, what do they mean? It is a comment, one not even phrased as a question and could mean many things, for instance:

- 'It is more than I expected.'
- 'It is more than current costs.'
- 'It is over the budget.'

- 'I'm not convinced it is value for money.'
- 'Can it be reduced?'
- 'I'm not clear what we get for it.'
- 'It is a lot to pay out at once.'
- 'Doesn't this rule other things out?'
- 'I don't understand.'
- 'I don't agree.'
- 'Can the methodology be changed to cut costs?'
- 'It needs more consideration.'
- 'It should not be done this year.'

You may be able to think of, or have experienced, more. Clearly many of these interpretations need answering along different lines; this example makes the point clearly that you have to understand exactly what is meant before you deal with it.

Secondly, if something is thrown out as a comment or challenge, just like *That is very expensive* in the above example, and in a form that is not a question, then it may be turned back to the questioner as a question to clarify. Thus it could be followed by the question: *Yes, it is a considerable cost, though I would suggest, of course, that it's a good investment, but what exactly are you saying? Is it more than the project warrants?* This kind of approach does a number of things quickly:

- It acknowledges the point (in the cost example, there is no merit in denying it is a great deal of money if someone clearly feels it is).
- It suggests you will be pleased to deal with the point.
- It makes your asking for more information about a concern seem helpful.

Once these preliminaries are out of the way, you can move on to actually addressing the objection. If you continue to keep in mind the image of a balance, referred to earlier, and bear in mind that there will be points – of varying importance and substance, on either side – then the job is one of ordering the balance, or reordering the one you have described, so that it presents a favourable basis for a positive decision, one that accepts the change (if not approving it 100 per cent). Sometimes, of course people will not agree even if the balance is positive; they are only going to agree if your described balance stacks up better than any different approach which they may also be evaluating.

You have four options in rebalancing:

1. Persuade objectors that their objection is false; in other words it exerts no weight on the minus side of the balance.
2. Concede that they have a point, but explain that the effect on the balance is minimal.
3. Concede completely and in this case – and the others – combine within your answer a re-emphasis on the plus points; that is the benefits that the change will bring.
4. Explain that the negative effect they see is actually a positive (something that is sometimes possible when there is significant misunderstanding).

This really is all that it is possible to do, so at least mechanistically the options are not too complicated. Complexity is added by the lead times and other matters involved in the project. For instance it may well be that a change is not seen through by one meeting of one group. The process of recognising and handling resistance may have to go on over a period of time and in a way that involves many different groups and individuals.

Essentially, the instigator of change must first identify why there is resistance: for example that people fear the change, the uncertainty, increased workload or complexity of operation and so on. Secondly, they must recognise that the answer may need to incorporate not only communication and explanation in all its forms, but also training, suggesting a shared vision and the involvement of people in various ways. One additional trick is to involve those who support change early on in the process to persuade others that it is necessary, good and should be accepted.

Overall, success is made more likely by going about things in the right way and orchestrating the whole approach. To summarise at this point remember the mnemonic SUCCESS:

- *Shared vision:* any change will go better if it fits with and is compatible with long-term goals and intentions.
- *Understanding of the organisation:* if the organisation is run to be 'fit for change' making changes will be easier and always how it is done must suit the organisation.
- *Culture compatibility:* the way people work and how they think is an important backdrop to any change.
- *Clear communication:* this is vital – throughout the process.
- *Expert assistance:* everyone involved must be equipped to play their part (and specialised help must be sought if needed to augment action for change).
- *Strong leadership:* the greater or more controversial the change the more it needs (firmly) directing from the top.
- *Stakeholder commitment:* must be understood and satisfying stakeholders built into any change.

Action

The most important lesson here is to ensure clear direction. Objectives must be spelt out, with people and processes well set up to see things through in the right way and to make sure that practicalities are accommodated and timings will work. This links in both directions: it is important to preparation and also to any action that is taken as things progress.

We now turn to more about communicating change in the next chapter.

4

Communicating change

Without a doubt change is better accepted and made if communication about it is good. If change is coming then people need to know about it. Just walking into the office one day to find something is radically different is likely to make most people unsettled and often resentful. How much people need to know, how far in advance, in what detail and so on depends on a number of factors, not least their proximity to the change: that is how much it will affect them or how they are involved in it. Clearly if people are involved in the implementation of change then they need to know and understand their role clearly and appropriately in advance.

The power of clarity

As the Roman general Quintilian said: 'One should not aim at being possible to understand, but at being impossible to misunderstand.' This is not necessarily easy; think how often you are involved in or overhear misunderstandings around your office. Any ambiguity can only cause trouble. If people do not understand they will be almost certain to fear the worst. Bad communication just *increases* the likelihood of negative attitudes being taken, of resistance and of rumour. It simply means that what can be a difficult process is made worse.

This is not the place for a complete run down on the techniques of communications but the following issues are worth mentioning:

- **All communication about change should be well considered. Take care and time and bear in mind the penalties of getting it wrong.**
- **Focus on your audience: whoever you are communicating with and their level of knowledge, experience and so on.**
- **Make sure language is appropriate: avoid unexplained jargon and follow the basic rules of clear, straightforward communication (for example, do not say 'at this moment in time' when you mean 'now').**
- **Consider building in checks, for instance getting written announcements read by someone other than whoever wrote them.**

If change affects a wide range of people then it may be necessary to communicate in different ways and to a different degree of detail with various separate groups of people. This may be more time consuming, but if one 'catch all' communication is likely to leave some people out in terms of complete understanding then the time taken to ensure all are suitably informed is only sensible.

The impact of culture

How communication is handled in general as much as in the face of change is dependent on the style of individual managers and executives and that, in turn, is influenced by the prevailing culture within the organisation. In some ways of course this is circular: the style and attitudes of senior people influence the culture; indeed such people actively influence the culture towards what they believe it should be.

The power of an organisation's culture is considerable. Culture is perhaps best defined as a combination of perceived best practice – *the way we do things round here* – and of commitment. It is perhaps difficult to define corporate culture, but it is something we all know when we meet it. It can easily be interpreted as the prevailing atmosphere at department level as well as more widely, and it is partly unspecific – it manifests itself as 'good feelings' in a variety of ways. But it is also very specific, can be very powerful and can certainly influence reactions.

For example, I can still remember being amazed by one particular aspect of the culture in the first consultancy firm I joined. It seemed anyone could walk into anyone else's office and ask for help; and they always received it. People might not drop everything and say, 'Sit down' instantly. They did, however, always offer something: 'Can you come back in half an hour?', 'How about getting together this afternoon?' For a newcomer, tackling new things and feeling my way, this was a godsend. I discovered that this attitude was encouraged – or rather actively fostered – by management (especially a few individuals), and maintained, not in any sense to conform but just because it worked. Everyone in the firm benefited. Two heads are better than one, and it was a business in which consultation, transfer of experience and discovering new creative approaches were essential. No one seemed to find themselves taking on an unrestricted or unreasonable burden by doing this. Everyone was involved and the load was shared. This is a clear example of the power of culture within an organisation, something being achieved not because of an instruction or system, but because of a common belief.

That said exactly *how* such belief is instilled is less clear. But it *is* possible so we need to consider how it might be achieved. Certainly unless change is recognised as demanding a very particular kind of communication then its smooth implementation and acceptance may be in jeopardy.

Setting the scene

Stay with culture for a moment: the first thing that needs to be said is that if positive aspects of culture are to be generated it needs commitment from the top. This may imply the chief executive, or simply the head of a department on a more 'local' scale. It is possible for useful practices to be initiated at grass roots level, of course, but difficult for them to stick and spread without support.

Usually the rationale is practical. In the example just given it was the nature of the consulting work that made working together so useful – brief, practical, mutual help sessions evolved because they enabled people to be productive and effective. Similarly a company may develop a strong feeling for customer service which stems primarily from a commonsense analysis of what is necessary, in a competitive world, to win and sustain business. So the starting point to creating an appropriate culture is an analysis of what needs to be achieved, and then what sort of behaviour is likely to assist the process.

When useful cultural behaviour begins to occur, it will be sustained better if it applies to everyone. Senior and less senior alike need to be involved (as was very much the case in my consultancy example); the behaviour of the senior people can then act as a role model for others. Their being seen to participate characterises the nature of the behaviour. It does not become 'something we are being asked (or told) to do'; rather it is seen as something most people seem to find desirable – and which works. At this point word of mouth about the usefulness of whatever it is often occurs and is an important way of keeping the pot boiling.

It is much easier to inject new information into a group who already regard themselves as well informed. Beyond any formal systems that may have a role to play, managers may want to look for ways to maintain or increase awareness of something, for example through items in company newsletters or on notice boards. Here the prospect of change should immediately flag the need for

communication and specifically for the need for systematic and
well considered communication at that. It should be a reflex.
It should be seen as essential and thus the time it takes to create
communication should not be seen as a chore, but as a necessity,
albeit one that is so because it is effective and useful.

It has been mentioned earlier that a natural human reaction
to change, especially an as yet undefined change, is suspicion and
a focus on possible – probable? – negative results. This fact can
cause problems: faced with this likely scenario some managers
have the instinctive view that secrecy is the answer: that little
should be said, at least until the very last minute. This instinct is
almost always wrong. Secrecy is likely to make people's reactions
more negative, so let's consider that for a moment first.

No secrets

One factor ranks high as a potential dampener of the acceptance
of change and that is secrecy; or rather it is *unnecessary* secrecy.
Some things of course do need, at particular times, to be kept
confidential. Exposing some changes too early can inform people
who will work against them. For instance a company does not
want a competitor to know about its intentions to launch a new
product as they may well be able to take spoiling action. That apart
a balance is necessary, simply because telling everyone everything
that goes on in a large organisation would be prohibitively time
consuming. However, people feeling that things – especially things
that might affect them – are being kept from them for no good
reason (or for patronising reasons – *they wouldn't understand*)
annoys and antagonises. Secrecy, that is manifestly unnecessary
secrecy, creates a culture of unease and wariness; and certainly
it makes acceptance of and involvement with change seem
undesirable and hinders the build-up of any behaviour or belief
that may be being encouraged to make it work.

On the other hand an open attitude, one that that staff
appreciate because it respects them, actively builds goodwill and

collaboration. In many organisations there is resentment about secrets that have no real need to be secrets. A little more communication can then change beliefs and behaviour and thus make it easier to plan and implement change.

As a (perhaps extreme) example of open management and a complete lack of secrecy, I know more than one organisation where all salaries are public knowledge. Anyone can walk into the accountant's office and ask what someone else is paid. No harm seems to be done. The greatest impact is on those responsible for deciding the level of salaries. It means that all differences – how one person's salary compares to another – must be explained if necessary. And that seem wholly right. The net result is that people *expect* all differentials to be fair. Attention to the policy means they are, in which case what is there to hide? I am *not* suggesting this would necessarily be right for every organisation. Yet it does certainly demonstrate that there may be many areas where reflexes dictate secrecy, yet where this is not actually important increased openness might well add something to the prevailing culture.

The moral is simple. Think carefully before you decide that 'no one needs to know'. Think about the timing, and build in a systematic element of keeping people involved and up to date. Many new developments are good. People will not only like to know about them, but also may be able to help, support or simply sing the praises of what is to come.

This does not apply to everything, of course. Some developments are bad. Some will affect people adversely. Even so, a news bombshell that only upsets will make it very difficult to carry people with you or to muster their support or cooperation. They resent not being informed. They feel it belittles them and their importance, and they react accordingly; and all this is on top of any tangible feelings that assess the change itself as in some way negative.

As a result coming change should prompt careful thinking about the communications aspect and how that, in turn, can help successful implementation.

Decisions about communication

You must think through and decide:

- who should be informed (and maybe who should not);
- when people should be informed;
- what they should be told;
- the method(s) of communication that are appropriate;
- how often they should be updated on progress or developments;
- the feedback mechanisms that need to be in place.

Above all you need to be sure that such communication makes it very clear *why* things are being done, and done in the way they are. Before dealing with these factors in turn, the process may need to address conflict, which may need nipping in the bud.

When conflict strikes

Realistically we must accept that groups of people do not always work amicably together. Sometimes there is friction. This can be constructive; it can prompt argument – discussion – and the process of ideas and counter ideas being thrown to and fro can result in useful outcomes, perhaps action and positive changes that would not have occurred otherwise.

But situations occur, especially when change is in the offing, where conflict overpowers sensible dialogue and argument. Sometimes negative feelings and emotion take over and the outcome is anything but amicable or constructive as people view a change and try to assess its likely effect on each of them. What causes this? Well, it may be a whole range of things beyond a normal apprehension about change. Perhaps something unreasonable has happened, perhaps people just dislike each other, but equally conflict may be evidence of a focus on personalities (rather than action), or on face-saving, the preservation of power or a need to 'get back at people' for some past real or imaginary upset or unfairness. This is human nature and can happen even in the best managed group, but it needs to be dealt with.

A manager has the role of peacemaker in such situations and the task of moving things on past the conflict and towards positive change. Faced with conflict between members of your team (or with others elsewhere in the organisation, perhaps another department), you must:

- **get to the root of the problem;**
- **keep calm and in control at all times;**
- **deal with things impartially;**
- **lay down clear rules of acceptable behaviour;**
- **deal with matters through discussion rather than argument.**

The processes and approaches involved then include:

- **Giving the matter adequate time; for example it may be necessary to see people separately first and, importantly for such meetings, to allow equal time with each individual (which will be read as fairness).**
- **Listening, and being seen to listen, carefully.**
- **Investigating and dealing with matters in the context of your underlying belief in the people concerned and also the benefits of any change that has caused or aggravated the conflict.**
- **Aiming to build bridges that will lead people away from conflict rather than attempt to magic problems away instantly, which may perhaps be unrealistic.**
- **Being careful throughout not to be censorious about matters (things that could seem silly to you, but seem overwhelmingly important to others).**

Resolving conflict

Conflict can all too often gradually build into major disruption. Small differences of opinion may start the process; then conflict escalates as people become defensive, aggressive or sometimes malicious. By the time it is clear that something must be sorted, positions are entrenched and it has become as much a battle of wills as a tangible problem. Even so discussion is the way out. It may help to see different people separately first to get their view, uninterrupted by argument. Then both, or all, parties need to sit down together and discuss the matter. Such a session calls for strong chairmanship and needs clear rules: for example only one person talking at a time, no interruptions, no insults (and a focus on the facts). You need to listen, make notes and recap regularly to be sure everyone moves forward together. A calm businesslike manner can be used to keep order and make it clear that the only route to resolution is going to be a rational one.

At the end of the day, people may have to agree to differ in some respects, but misunderstandings should be ironed out and the need to work amicably together must be shown to override what may come to be seen as unimportant petty squabbling.

In such circumstances, the heat has to be taken out of the situation and this may mean curtailing argument and reconvening when tempers have calmed. Most people are embarrassed by conflict, theirs and other people's (it is uncomfortable being on the sidelines of arguments, especially if invited to take sides). Ultimately therefore people will return to more rationale ways of dealing with matters and your guidance and role as peacemaker must encourage this.

At the end of the day people must work together. Transient problems can usually be resolved. Realistically, occasionally you may need to take action that removes an interface that manifestly has no hope of existing peacefully and constructively. This might be done by reorganisation, and could – if someone's behaviour warrants it – result in dismissal. These days few organisations can sensibly accommodate someone who always takes irrationally against any proposed change and who escalates any hint of it into conflict. Usually such matters can be resolved, often they prove to be storms in teacups (though they still need sensitive handling even then) and clear rules of behaviour should ensure that matters rarely get to a really difficult stage.

There is merit in being seen as firm in sticking to rules (which can be informal yet given weight), sensitive in handling matters of conflict yet focused on ensuring a belief that the prime objective is action to ensure work is completed satisfactorily.

A systematic approach

We return now to the list of six positive measures that change necessitates in terms of communication (whether what is being communicated is good or bad news).

1. Who should be informed (and maybe who should not)

Given the problem of people feeling alienated by being 'kept in the dark' as they would see it, you perhaps need to resolve to communicate with everyone in any way involved. This should include anyone who has any role in what will follow (even in an intangible sense – for instance asking who might spread positive, negative or inaccurate messages about what is happening). It is better to over-broaden the population with which you communicate than risk people feeling left out. Perhaps it helps to start from the other end in your assessment and ask who definitely has no interest in or need for the information.

2. When people should be informed

The rule here is to communicate promptly. However, having said that, matters must be at a stage where there is something definite to say; though once it is clear something is going on, a preliminary announcement may help even if it is clearly not the full picture. In this case it is always more acceptable if the fact that there is more to come is made clear and the timescale is indicated as far as possible. Then, if you say that there will be a further announcement by the end of the month, make one. Even a few days beyond what is expected – or promised – will be resented and rumours, mainly negative ones, will begin to fly.

Additionally, aim to tell everyone affected at the same time. Again rumours will fly around if one group is informed and others are not (but quickly grasp that 'something is up'). There may be a stage when some people who will be key players in a project must be briefed ahead of, or in more detail than, others. If so then this must be done very carefully. Make sure that no external announcement of anything is ahead of internal ones. Even something like a sales person having a new advertisement pointed out to them by a customer when they have seen and heard nothing of it internally may cause embarrassment and thus resentment.

A suggestion here is to link one announcement to another. For example, if a company's results are announced then news of a change may be linked to that in a way that allows the first, more general announcement to set the scene. Good results lead logically to changes to take the organisation forward further; bad ones need action to redress the situation. Change then at least has a real logic locked in up front.

3. What they should be told

The rule here is to tell people sufficient detail to make sense and carry them with you, and almost always this is made better by your being sure that *why* something is done is well explained. For example, a change to customer service methodology may be planned to keep up with or overtake competitors. If so then that should come first, then the details of whatever it is that will actually be done in terms of practice or procedure can be taken in context with the reason behind it already made clear.

That said, time makes a good basis on which to divide matters up: tell people what is planned (and why), tell them what is happening now and spell out what will happen next, if necessary with a timetable to give details.

4. How often they should be updated on progress or developments

The timetable just mentioned ties in here. The scale of changes varies greatly. A change may be a one-off action implemented overnight, or it could be a multi-stage process spanning many weeks or months (or longer).

The timetable needs to provide a thread to this when the timescale is longer. Think of the perspective of those involved. A manager may be paid to think in terms of financial years and long-term planning, but someone in the sales or packing department may think next Friday is long term. Regular updates in light of assessing the people involved in this way are important, and it is useful too if this is flagged ahead – *I'll update you in three weeks' time.*

5. Appropriate method(s) of communication

A variety of methods can be deployed to act in support of the communications you need to make. The following are examples and you may well be able to think of more. Consider:

- *Meetings:* **staff meetings, project meetings, even company-wide conferences can all have an element that announces change – either of itself or linked to reporting successes, looking ahead and so on. These days virtual meetings (for example, from video presentations to webinars online) – ways of communicating with people without their all being gathered together – are a viable** option. As meetings are so important, and many changes require communicating with people face to face, the box below offers some guidelines.

- *Individual briefings:* these may be necessary for staff specifically affected or who will be involved in implementation.
- *Specific memos:* most often this now means emails and that may be fine unless the nature of the change is sensitive (think of the furore that always accompanies anyone being fired by email). Sometimes a greater formality may be necessary and it is worth asking people to print something out and keep it or circulating a paper copy as well as or instead of an email
- *Newsletters:* indeed any regular missive can be part of documenting changes (this includes such devices as notice boards and methods such as e-newsletters).
- *Social activities:* these too can play a part and gatherings can be designed to achieve a specific purpose (for example, mixing two departments) provided the social element does not suffer or the event end up being seen as contrived. For example, someone's retirement party might be a good occasion for an appropriately couched first announcement to flag reorganisation that will follow the retiree's departure.

Making meetings work

Meetings are ubiquitous. But they can be hard work, difficult, boring and too often end up serving no useful purpose and neither advancing things nor prompting decisions. No wonder that it is said that the ideal meeting is 'two, with one absent'.

Meetings are the archetypal mixed blessing. They are time consuming (and thus cost money), and yet they *are* an important part of organisational communications, consultation, debate and decision making; thus they are often vital to the change process. Yet good, effective meetings do not just happen. No deep law of meetings means putting up with bad ones in order to get an occasional good one thrown in, and a culture of effective meetings will not exist unless everyone in an organisation actively works at it. Everybody's role is important, whether running a meeting or attending one. When change is to be made you cannot afford for a poor meeting (and poor communication) to blight the chances of people understanding and accepting what is to come.

The best of meetings

Whatever the meeting, large or small, formal or informal, long or short, if it is planned, considered and conducted specifically to make it go well, then it can be made effective, whatever its purpose. Meetings can seek to do a number of things: inform, analyse and solve problems, discuss and exchange views, inspire and motivate, counsel and reconcile conflict, obtain opinion and feedback, persuade, train and develop, reinforce the status quo, impress and progress change in a variety of ways.

One key purpose is to prompt action in a range of ways from simply understanding change to actively supporting it and playing a part in making it happen. Additionally good meetings are not just useful; they can stimulate creative discussion and action that would never occur unless a particular group got together, surely an inherent part of identifying areas for change.

First base

For a meeting to be truly successful, ensuring its success cannot begin only as the meeting starts – the 'I think we're all here, what shall we deal with first?' attitude. Making it work starts before the meeting, sometimes some time before.

First, ask some basic questions, for example: is a meeting really necessary? Should it be one of a series of meetings? Think carefully here: you do not want to waste time with too many but regular updates may oil the wheels as a change is underway. Who should attend? (And who should not?).

If you are clear in these respects then you can proceed. Some key points to bear in mind include:

1. *Setting an agenda:* this is very important – no meeting will go as well if you simply make up the content as you get under way (notify the agenda in advance and give good notice of any contributions required from others).

2. *Timing:* set a meeting start time *and* a finishing time, then you can judge its conduct alongside the duration and even put some rough timings to individual items to be dealt with. Respect the timing too: always start on time and try to stick within the planned duration.

3. *Objective:* always set a clear objective – in advance – so that you can state clearly *why* a meeting is being held.

4. *Prepare yourself:* read all necessary papers, check all necessary details and think about how you will handle both your own contribution and the stimulation, and control, of others.

5. *Insist others prepare also:* this may mean instilling habits (if you pause to go through something that should have been studied before the meeting, then preparation is immediately seen as not really necessary and this may affect future meetings).

6. *People:* what roles individuals attending should have.

7. *Environment:* a meeting will work best if people attending are comfortable: so organise for no interruptions and switch the coffee pot on and the phones off.

Then, at the appointed hour, you must take charge and make the meeting go well (and something else to bone up on may be the skills of good chairmanship).

There is a real opportunity here: communication is vital to the change process and where it takes place in this manner it must be done well.

Other methods may be involved at early stages when consultation is occurring. For example:

- *Suggestions schemes:* **often much maligned, these can be a very useful spur to involvement** *provided* **there is good feedback and credit (and perhaps reward) is given appropriately and fairly. An early announcement might thus be linked to a request for specific kinds of suggestion ahead of a coming change.**
- *Quality circles:* **the (Japanese originated) system of meetings and exchanges designed to improve quality can in fact be focused on any topic (including specific areas like customer care procedures) and be made to be seen as a useful – and regular – element of communications; again such might be given a particular emphasis ahead of changes to come.**
- *Brainstorming:* **useful to discover hidden possibilities for positive change: more of this in a page or two.**

In all such communication there is a need to focus on the positive. There are always two ways of looking at everything: the classic glass half full or empty description. It is important that a message comes over in a way that increases optimism and prompts the action or support that circumstances make necessary. For example, something like a move to new premises may spark dread: the upheaval, the backlog of work, the worry about 'my new location' and uncertainties about conditions and facilities. The communication can counter this by focusing on the positive:

an opportunity to reorganise, an improved image for the company or department, better conditions of work for people, how the plan will minimise difficulties and the underlying reason why it is necessary (which might be growth, success and an opportunity to expand further in future).

No one wants to work for a manager who is all doom and gloom; indeed the attitude may prove contagious and create a culture of 'seeing problems everywhere'. As a manager you need to develop a firm habit of thinking before you speak in this respect, analysing both sides of any situation and putting problems in perspective by stressing the positive side and the positive results to be aimed for at the end of the day. Change is certainly an area where accentuating the positive is likely to make getting through the change that much easier.

6. Exercising appropriate methods of control

Clearly someone needs to be in charge – to wear the 'change hat' as it were. Others may be involved if major multi-faceted change is involved but control should be delegated downwards and one person may need to keep a total overview with regard to communications.

7. Having appropriate feedback mechanisms in place

There is all the difference in the world between a bald announcement and a consultation. If consultation is appropriate it must be seen to happen, and seen to make a difference. Even if consultation is not appropriate or happened at an earlier stage or in a different way, communication about changes is an opportunity for (further) feedback. Sometimes in the haste of complex processes it is forgotten to canvass views. It is rightly said that the nice thing about good ideas is that they do not care who has them. Many a manager has been surprised by how many suggestions they get from down the line if they ask – and how sensible they often are. So in the circumstances of change do not forget to make it easy for people to provide feedback or ideas and that the email address, or whatever, that makes it possible is clearly included. One specific method of unearthing ideas, which was mentioned earlier, is that of brainstorming (see the box below).

Brainstorming: guidelines for success

Brainstorming is a group activity and can be used to provide an almost instant burst of idea generation. It can work well when change is actively sought and especially when there is no consensus as to what should be done. Working with a group of people (maybe three or four but up to a dozen works easily), it needs a prescribed approach to ensure creativity:

- **Gather people around and explain the objectives clearly (everyone wants to know exactly what ideas are required and why).**
- **Explain that there are to be *no comments* on ideas at this initial stage.**
- **Allow a little time for thought (singly or perhaps in pairs).**
- **Start taking contributions and noting them down (publicly on say a flipchart).**
- **When a good-sized list is established and recorded, then analysis can begin.**
- **Grouping similar ideas together can make the list more manageable.**
- **Open-minded discussion can then review the list.**
- **Identify ideas for change that can be taken forward.**

Such a session must exclude the word 'impossible' from the conversation, at least initially – and especially when used in contexts such as *It's impossible; we don't do things that way* (Why not?), or *It's impossible; we tried it once and it didn't work.* (How long ago and in what form?).

By avoiding any negative or censorious first responses, by allowing one idea to spark another and variations on a theme to refine a point (perhaps taking it from something wild to something practical), a brainstorming session can produce genuinely new approaches and be a useful catalyst in prompting change.

It can also be fun to do, satisfying in outcome and time-efficient to undertake – and members of a group who brainstorm regularly get better at it, and quicker and more certain in their production of good, useable, ideas.

Do not forget to give credit for any good ideas that are input; it is a good opportunity to inject a little positive motivation. This can be as simple as a well placed *Well done!* Or, at the other end of the scale, it could be an incentive payment or reward scheme of some sort.

It is too easy for a lack of encouragement to stifle the flow of ideas and for things that could be very useful to be missed. This can happen in the simplest ways and it is important to maintain an atmosphere that promotes suggestion at every level. For example, a company developed a new treatment for mouth ulcers. As for any medicine this had to be tested. Clinical trials were set up and, as usual, a panel of doctors was briefed to prescribe the gel and report back. Reports were few and far between and deadlines for the launch process drew nearer with no prospect of the trial concluding in time. It was the department's secretary that suggested that patients were surely much more likely to mention their problem to a dentist rather than a doctor. A new trial was quickly instigated and results came in promptly and provided sufficient positive evidence for the product to be launched (on time). This story was told to me by the secretary who had considered for a while before saying anything: the solution seemed so obvious and she felt that 'Surely they would have thought of it, and I did not want to look silly.' The day was saved, but a quick solution to the problem was very nearly missed. Surely every organisation wants management to encourage every kind of suggestion in such circumstances and be equally grateful for every one, whether they prove useful or not.

Empowerment

In the vast majority of work places telling people what to do is no longer a main element of management. Teams of people are most productive (in every sense) when they have a reasonable degree of self-sufficiency. If changes either continue to allow the existing degree of empowerment or increase it, this fact is certainly worth stating. People want to take ownership and they want to feel they are 'in charge', if not of the whole organisation, at least of their own area or activity.

Sometimes controls and the need for tight supervision are perpetuated only because there is an assumption that they are necessary. Times and circumstances change; perhaps something was once necessary but that does not mean it must continue forever. For example, I remember analysing a situation in a client company some years ago. A particular decision (linked to product exchange and return) reflected the policy that could be adopted with regard to customers. Such product exchange had to be checked with a supervisor. This took time (which cost money) and reduced the speed of customer service as staff went to and fro to find and discuss the matter with their supervisor. But management felt that supervisor input was important. So we monitored separately the decisions the supervisors made alongside those the staff said they would make if allowed to do so. The views of what action should be taken were almost always identical. In other words the delay, the check or the consultation did not affect the action. Instead it just took time, money and reduced customer service. The check was discontinued, and customer service improved. So too did motivation, as people felt trusted and liked taking responsibility and relying on their own judgement. This was not a change that was difficult to sell to the staff involved precisely because it increased their empowerment. The facts of the study enhanced their self-esteem and helped convince the supervisors.

Such situations are not uncommon. You need to think about the attitude you take to giving people their heads and letting them take responsibility for their own actions. Setting up how things will work, briefing people and, if necessary, giving them the authority and the knowledge to act alone is necessary first, but a manager should surely aim at creating a high level of self-sufficiency wherever possible. Such an attitude can foster useful ongoing change.

Making it work

Everything that has been discussed in this chapter is easier for the individual manager to achieve if there is a culture in the organisation that is supportive of good staff communications. In fact, culture goes further than this. It initiates and maintains action and fosters ongoing attitudes and work habits that make efficiency and effectiveness more likely.

This is not something that you can afford only to respond to. Time and events will create some sort of corporate culture. The only question is what will do so and what will be the nature of the culture thus created. Managers have a responsibility to influence the culture, indeed to consider what it should comprise, and actively aim to create what is most helpful. On the other hand if the lead here comes from the top, so much the better. If not you, and others, may need to take an initiative both in creating and maintaining a culture positive to change and perhaps also encouraging senior management to play their part. (This latter aspect may be a longer-term educational process, dare I say, given the intransigence of some senior managers.)

One thing is certain: culture affects the success of communications and communications affect the results to be achieved through change.

Action

Whenever change is in the offing, thinking about communication and a systematic approach to it, not least an approach that appears open and respects those involved, will always smooth the path. Think about the issues ahead of action – this will make a considerable difference. Forward thinking is a prime thread running through the whole process so should never be skimped but done well.

Change in practice

The range of areas over which change holds sway has already been made clear from what has been written earlier, and it is thus impossible to encompass every possible kind of change in illustrating how it can be made to happen. However, in this chapter three examples are investigated in a little more detail. These are chosen so that they are as different from each other as possible but are relevant to most readers.

The first is unsurprisingly from the area of information technology. It is an area where few of us need reminding of the rate of change occurring or the need to keep up to date. The second concerns an underrated technique linked to making personal change, and the third illustrates the sheer complexity sometimes involved.

Example 1: changing technology (QR codes)

One area where rapid change is all too apparent is in the area of technology and of information technology (IT) in particular. Ever since computers found themselves on every desk in the land things have changed. Take customer service: those receiving queries or orders from customers used to work manually. Holding on the phone while someone in the sales office got your file out of a filing cabinet was normal. Now it is all different. Once you are through, simply stating your post code brings up your address on screen in an instant and, at best, matters can be dealt with very speedily. But the transition involved for such a department is considerable and it has made those without suitable computer skills, or the ability to acquire them fast, out of a job.

The example of Quick Response (QR) codes illustrates the IT example well. Such devices are reasonably new and for those unfamiliar with them an example is shown in Figure 5.1. This is the QR code that actually appears and is related to this book.

Figure 5.1   This book's QR code

QR codes look somewhat like the bar codes that appear on so many products and which prompt a beep as they are scanned in a supermarket. They generate the receipt (and link to the store's stock and accounting systems, customer records, special offers, reward points and more).

So, what exactly are QR codes? Simply they are a means of communication. They can be accessed by any smart phone equipped with the right 'app': that is an application that scans the code and which can then connect to a wireless network and specifically open a web page on the phone to allow the user to view information. To get the inevitable jargon out of the way, this is known as a hardlink or physical world hardlink. Many smart phones already have the necessary app as standard and this trend will no doubt continue. (The QR reader is widely available, though there are other systems and the ultimate standard may not have settled yet.)

QR codes are (as I write) beginning to appear all over the place: on products, in shop windows, on posters and advertising materials of all sorts – catch a bus in Paris and a QR code at the bus stop can tell you which bus to take and how long it will be before the next one arrives. By the time you read this, they may well be truly ubiquitous. If you have a phone that will link to it, you can try out the one in this book (though maybe after you have read on a little further). So why put one on a book? With a book in front of you this makes a good example (though such a device will have different purposes in different circumstances).

Given the technology, and however much matters may have moved on since I wrote this, imagine it is new. A key application is in marketing: so what should a book publisher do? Should they utilise this technology and, if so, why and what might they get from it? Imagining the thinking involved here is a good example of one aspect of handling change – assessing its relevance and potential usefulness ahead of any deployment of it.

So how can a QR code help sell a book? First consider how a non-fiction book is bought; you may recognise here something of how you got hold of this one.

The purchaser weighs it up; we only buy anything when we assess there is a good case for it. Such weighing up may take just a second or two in a supermarket or some days if you are buying say a new car. In the case of this book, assuming that the topic is relevant and that someone wants or needs to know about it, they need to form a view that this is 'the one for them' (after all few books are the sole reference on a subject). Thus they look at, and assess, a variety of things. The weight and usefulness of these in terms of their influence on the decision will vary and some examples of what may be considered, in no particular order, include: the front cover design and information, the author, the publisher and endorser, the blurb, its apparent accessibility, whether any key words or headings jump out as useful, the publication date, the price, the length, sample text and not least reviews on the inside or the jacket.

The detail of all of these may be important too. For example, has the author written other books (this one has), is the book part of a series and have you read others in it, do you know something about a reviewer, respect them or simply find what they say informative? All such factors, and more, contribute to someone deciding that the title will be useful and moving on to purchase it.

But a QR code in a book adds to all this. For the prospective buyer needing more information or simply liking technology and wanting to check out how it works in a specific application, finding out more is quick and easy. The QR code may link someone to the publisher's website, where they might find additional information; illustrations linked to the book; background about the author; information about the range of titles published; opportunities to sign up to receive newsletters and promotional offers; any (further) reviews; downloadable extracts; and online resources such as podcasts.

Some of this information may help someone make a quick judgement, while other aspects of it may be of long-term interest or something to return to later. In addition there may need to be a facility for feedback and (easy) ordering.

A further opportunity is that the code can be more widely visible than on the book itself: it may be visible on another book, alongside a review in a magazine, on promotional material or in a publisher's newsletter.

The process involved here is clear. First, the change has
to be recognised and recognised as an opportunity. Then the
implications have to be thought through:

- **A QR code must be originated.**
- **An easy visible prompt on the website it links to must
  flag up the specific additional detail (and also lead
  elsewhere if appropriate).**
- **Individual 'pieces' of information (be they text, video
  or whatever) must be created.**
- **A greater, and perhaps more regular, update procedure
  must be put in place so that the website is always
  spot on.**
- **A monitoring process must be in place too (not
  least to count usage: there is no point in spending
  marketing resources on something that people do not
  look at – so, particularly in the early days, testing is
  necessary).**
- **The whole marketing mix may need reassessment
  either because more time, effort and money spent on
  this allows less to be expended on other activities, or
  because particular factors need to change (perhaps
  pricing is affected, for instance) or new links between
  the new technology and others are necessary.**

A whole separate element also comes into play here, that of
personnel. Who is going to do these things? Will their skills
enable them to do so and do so well? If the responsibilities of
people change there may be a domino effect: John does this,
so Mary must take over that, etc but you get the picture.

Such an example shows up the whole process. A sequence is
involved:

- **A change needs to be recognised (in this case a
  technological one).**
- **The technology itself must be understood.**
- **Any opportunity presented must be recognised.**

- The potential advantage must be analysed: what will need to be done, how can it be done, who will do it, what will it cost? And more.
- The implications for change elsewhere must be considered, in budgets, activity and so on.
- If the assessment is positive a plan must be prepared and sanctioned.
- Implementation must be set in motion, managed and monitored.
- Long-term results must be assessed and ongoing fine-tuning of practice undertaken to maximise success over time.

Throughout all this communication is going to be important too. In every case the overall nature of the change must be borne in mind. For instance in the case of QR codes the ultimate impact is on customers, so customer service and satisfaction must be paramount throughout the process; and ultimately so must profitability as this is essentially a marketing initiative.

Beware the clash of old and new

I think two dangers stand out clearly from what has been said here. First, there is the danger of procrastination and thus ignoring new things and failing to maximise an opportunity. I am not suggesting that everything needs rushing into; things must be well worked out and executed thoroughly (and only when judged appropriate). But operational matters are uppermost in most people's minds, so there is often a clash between the time that is spent just keeping a department, operation or organisation running effectively and finding time to consider and implement changes. A balance must be struck here and it may need organising so that some time *is* dedicated to new activities. The second danger is that too much time and effort are spent investigating potential changes and current operations suffer as eyes are 'taken off the ball'.

Action

The QR code shown in Figure 5.1 is real. If you have a smart phone try linking to it and see how it introduces you to the Kogan Page website. Seeing this in action may prompt you to consider using the code in your own situation or business.

Example 2: changing people (mentoring)

In Chapter 6 we investigate personal aspects of change and how everybody needs to keep up to date, develop new skills and ensure that they are able to do the job they want or need to do, both current and future. The phrase 'life-long learning' came into the business lexicon a while ago and it is surely apparent to all that standing still in today's fast changing world is a recipe for disaster.

People have to change. If you are a manager you may have to change people and you yourself must surely change too in terms of what you do and how you do it. Here I have picked as an example something that is often an underrated agent for change, and focus on a particular and personal technique: that of mentoring. It is a powerful and useful technique, and provides another, rather different, example of the change process.

Mentoring

A mentor is someone who exercises a low-key and informal developmental role. One of the motivations for a manager, or at least for some managers, is the satisfaction of helping people develop, succeed and do well as a result. I was, looking back on my career, very lucky in that two of the people I worked for early on were brilliant examples of this. I learned a great deal from both and learned it very much quicker than would otherwise have been the case. I am not, on the other hand, at all sure that if I had not had this luck I would have had the wits to seek out such assistance. I suspect that my career planning may have been too naïve in the earliest days of my career. The fact is that mentoring can add to other ongoing activities and enhance the amount and precision of development for an individual. But how does mentoring work?

More than one person can be involved in the mentoring of a single individual and, while what they do is akin to some of the things a line manager should do, more typically in terms of how the word is used a mentor is specifically *not* your line manager. It might be someone more senior, someone on the same level or from elsewhere in the organisation or indeed from outside it. An effective mentor can be a powerful force in any individual's development. Let's look at it personally: it could be useful. So how do you get yourself a mentor?

In some (usually larger) organisations mentoring is a regular part of ongoing development. You may be allocated one or able to request one. Equally you may need to act to create a mentoring relationship for yourself (something that may demand some persuasion). You can suggest it to your manager, or direct to someone you think might undertake the role, and take the initiative.

What makes a good mentor? The person must:

- **have authority (this might mean they are senior, or just that they are capable and confident);**
- **have suitable knowledge and experience, counselling skills and appropriate clout;**
- **be willing to spend some time with you (their doing this with others may be a positive sign).**

Finding time may be a challenge for both parties. One way to minimise that problem is to organise mentoring on a swap basis: someone agrees to help you and you line up your own manager (or you for that matter) to help them, or one of their people.

However it is set up, a series of informal meetings can result, together creating a thread of activity through the regular operational round. These meetings need an agenda (or at least an informal one), but more importantly they need to be constructive. If they are, then one thing will naturally lead to another and a variety of occasions can be utilised to maintain the dialogue. A meeting – followed by a brief encounter as people pass on the stairs – a project and a promise to spend a moment on feedback – an e-mail or two passing in different directions – all may contribute. Consider an example.

If someone needs to develop presentational skills then they need to understand what is necessary to create a good presentation and also to practise. A mentor can help with both aspects of the process. For instance the two parties might go through the following sequence of events:

1. First, the problem needs to be identified: regular mentoring meetings may help here, the mentor may have observed the need or it may be raised to them as a problem.
2. To make progress understanding must come first. The mentor could take time to brief their charge, suggest a course to attend or a book to read.
3. The next time a presentation must be done, it can be reviewed at preparation stage. This can lead to a second round of more focused preparation and to an improved presentation ready to be made.
4. The mentor is a captive audience, so the next step might be a rehearsal, something that always helps and can lead to further fine tuning.
5. The mentor may then be able to attend the actual presentation (though not intervening on the day).

6. After the presentation has been made there can be a post-presentation review that points up lessons for next time.
7. The involvement can run on: more help with preparation, more rehearsals and so on as experience builds.

None of this takes an undue amount of time; indeed much of it is only time that would be taken anyway but with a mentor's involvement added. It is evolution rather than revolution; it gradually nudges the person towards a better and better informed way of doing things and then builds on success. The good mentor will do this in a positive and constructive way too, not simply criticising (though some constructive criticism may be necessary), but identifying and building on strengths and encouraging and motivating.

The steps above do not represent a definitive list; various variations are possible, as are more or less time and involvement. Indeed whether you are a mentor or aim to mentor others (and it is certainly a way to promote and ensure change) you can see how such an approach can be tailored to fit the circumstances and the time.

What makes the mentoring process useful is the commitment and quality of the mentor. Where such relationships can be set up, and where they work well, they add a powerful dimension to the ongoing cycle of development, one that it is difficult to imagine being bettered in any other way.

Overall, what you learn from the ongoing interactions and communications you have with your line manager and others such as a mentor can be invaluable. It may leave some matters to be coped with in other ways, but it can prove the best way to deal with many matters and also to add useful reinforcement in areas of development that also need a more formal approach. As both parties become familiar with the arrangement and how it works, and with each other, it can become highly productive. Having been lucky enough to have someone in this role myself for many years I well know that often just a few minutes spent together can crack a problem or lead to a new initiative.

Good idea

A mentor is usually taken to be someone senior (and/or more experienced) to the person to whom they act as mentor. But a similar relationship is possible with colleagues (for example, other members of your team or department). There is no reason why you cannot forge a number of useful and reciprocal alliances, perhaps each designed to help in rather different ways.

Mentoring is often an underrated methodology – one that can add solid ongoing change over a period of time and focus that change in any way that may be necessary. It is well worth investigating, experimenting with and using.

Mentoring can affect personal change (linked to career change) very well. New skills and processes are involved and getting to grips with them has to precede getting into a new area of work and cope with it. Whatever the circumstances – you may want to take on new tasks, new responsibilities whether to enhance your existing job or better fit you for another involving an upward step – such action may be necessary. Whatever that involves, and mentoring or training are just two possible actions, setting things up correctly makes sense and makes success both more likely and possibly earlier than would an ad hoc approach. Usually, if such a relationship lasts, it will start out one way – the mentor helps you – but it can become more two-way over time; perhaps a potential mentor makes the decision to help on the basis of this possibility. Indeed if a two-way aspect of the process is encouraged then still more change can result.

Once this is up and running, there is no reason why someone cannot have regular contact with a number of people where in each case the relationship is of this nature. This can take various forms. In my own case, for instance, my work in marketing overlaps sometimes with the area of market research. While I know a good deal about aspects of this, certainly in terms of what can be done with it, I have no real strength in the statistical techniques involved. But I have a research mentor: someone who can help and advise me in this particular field. This is very useful and works on the basis of a swap; in other words he helps me in that way and I am able (I hope) to advise and assist him in other ways. This is a not uncommon basis.

At the risk of repetition, mentoring is an important and oft neglected agent for change. It may be low key, indeed that is one of its strengths, but it can be very powerful on an ongoing basis. For many people it is well worth checking out.

Example 3: moving

As a final example, to give a snapshot of the realities of change, here is something that illustrates the sheer logistical problem some kinds of change involve: the situation of moving offices. This is a complicated business and a chore even when it is undertaken for the best possible reasons, perhaps growth and the need to accommodate an increasing number of people as operations expand.

We will skip any details of the first stage, but that is not to minimise what is involved in it, and assume the decision to move is for positive reasons. Selecting where to move to, followed by all the legal detail of leases, purchasing or whatever is involved requires professional advice so whoever is undertaking this stage may need to work with estate agents, surveyors, legal people and also various contractors (builders, electricians and so on) if any work is needed to fit the new premises to their new occupants. So with new premises set up and ready, what about the actual process of moving?

How it will be seen

Anyone who has moved house, and most who have not, assume the whole process will be a nightmare. They will anticipate disruption and personal inconvenience and they will be fearful for themselves: wondering if they are going to be placed in some dark basement, with bad lighting, cramped conditions and a mile to walk to the photocopier or coffee machine.

As a result communications are particularly important here (yes, again). Those faced with such a move not only need to know what is happening, how it will affect them and what they must do, but also need their fears allayed. If it is in fact a good move they need to be enthused to see it as such. This is the kind of event about which rumours will start very early in the process, so communications must start from day one and be clear and honest as matters progress. Specifically people will need to be told up front:

- *Why a move is being made:* **here a positive slant should surely be put on everything and it may help to link an initial announcement to details of what consultation has been (or will be) involved. It can encourage unease if it is seen only as something management says 'must be done'.**
- *What the benefits are to both individuals and the organisation:* **these need to be spelt out separately and also linked: so that if the move is facilitating growth then this is described as both benefiting the company and its staff (members of which may have better pay, prospects or security if growth is made possible).**
- *What any snags may be:* **here there is a need to be honest. For example, if the new location is some distance away and people's journey to work is affected, then it should not be said that it will add only 10 minutes to a journey, when it is actually 20 and on London's notorious M25.**

- *And where the move is being made to:* **an address of course, but also maps and details of the locality – everything from cafes, libraries or schools to transportation and car parking.**

An 'all things to all people' approach to communications can often be inappropriate and satisfy no one, so separate tailored communications may need to go to different individuals and groups. As decisions are made and arrangements come together, regular communications are going to be necessary (at best such a move may take months). A plethora of details will progressively need communicating about when the move will take place, how long it will take and (on an individual basis) where people will be located. Much of this will be action orientated, for instance specifying what people need to do to contribute to the packing process.

Meantime there are a whole lot of arrangements to be made. The following gives a flavour of what's involved.

What goes where

Perhaps this heading should read 'Who and what go where': the two go together. Different people need a different environment and equipment, from customer service staff that spend all day on the telephone in front of a computer screen to design staff, where perhaps people need more space and exceptional lighting.

Deciding such placement needs careful consideration (and likely consultation too). Which areas might be visited by outsiders such as customers? What's the relationship between people, their roles and the equipment they use? (Given the amount of electronic equipment in most offices the wiring and links are a major consideration). Is any new furniture necessary (and if so who gets it)? Such a list of considerations is long and sensibly includes both tangible factors and others such as how communications and social interactions will work.

In addition, the question of whether things are just changing location or changing in nature needs deciding and accommodating; for instance, a department in which everyone had an individual work station or desk may now become a hot-desking area.

The move

Packing and moving need some organising, removal specialists no doubt need hiring and although they will do the physical work and do so expertly and safely if they are well chosen, there are other matters to be considered. Such include deciding an order in which things will be done: for instance, here it may be that departments like customer services need to be given priority to minimise any period when they are out of action or on reduced operations. Another consideration is specialist equipment: even computer systems may need separate professional help to move them safely and preserve their warranties.

Interim arrangements

It would be nice to think that operations close down on Friday afternoon in one place and resume on a normal basis on Monday morning. More likely there will need to be interim arrangements for a short period as things settle. If this means something like reduced customer service or delayed deliveries, then this needs to be thought through, customers notified and even compensated. Equally marketing might see it as an opportunity – communicating to pull orders forward or offering special terms during the interim. Again a positive slant needs to be put on all this, communicating a clear indication of how things will ultimately be better than before the move.

And finally

The main headings above only scratch the surface and it is not the intention here to actually brief you about moving offices.

However let's add a few other details to show the extent of the matter:

- **Public announcement:** this may involve a press release, notification of customers and everything from printing new letterhead and stationery to updating a corporate website and organising new maps to show the organisation's location.
- **Staff information:** not just communication in written form about the plan, but advice (for instance about local schools) and even one-to-one counselling about individual situations.
- **Inspection visits:** for instance by staff ahead of the actual move.
- **Standing instructions:** instructions need to be prepared for staff about working in the new premises: everything from safety rules to not using the customer reception or showroom as a rest room.
- **New staff arrangements:** for instance a dedicated bus service may be laid on to collect staff from some central point near the old premises and take them to the new (such ideas can assist with another consideration, that of staff retention).
- **Contractual arrangements:** for instance what happens if for personal reasons a member of staff cannot reasonably move or if a long-distance move involves people in significant cost?
- **Servicing and suppliers:** perhaps depending on the distance moved, new arrangements may need to be made with suppliers or new ones appointed: everything from who runs the canteen and the delivery of mail to who cleans the offices or services the photocopiers.

As a further point, remember that despite all the physical matters to be attended to, some of the thoughts of staff will reflect intangible matters. For instance, there may be problems relating to the status considerations of who sits where and who has their own individual office, perhaps. Whoever is making the arrangements cannot afford to be censorious: things that are unimportant to them may worry others and throughout the moving process people must be motivated to see it all as necessary, good and to be cooperated with in every way.

Implications

This example is chosen not least to illustrate the complexities: here in terms of things to be done, people involved and potential difficulties over the time that the planning and executing of a move will inevitably take. Various actions seem necessary; indeed all the examples here make a more general point:

- **A 'stage manager' is needed to coordinate everything and everyone involved.**
- **Consultation is surely necessary, particularly as everyone is involved in this case.**
- **Individual roles must be clearly defined and individuals well briefed about them.**
- **Communication must start early, be clear, precise, specific and honest and continue regularly through the process.**
- **Motivation as well as information will be necessary to ensure a smooth transition.**
- **A time line must be established to ensure everything links and runs smoothly together.**
- **As well as planning what should happen, some contingency is sensible and it must be clear where lines of decision lie if unforeseen events make any fine-tuning necessary along the way.**

Appropriate consultation

It is worth picking up on one matter arising from the point about consultation in the list above. This concerns the concept of democracy. Consultation is certainly important, and in the modern workplace it is also expected: people resent something apparently just thrust upon them, especially if it appears to ignore matters of importance to them. Yet there needs to be a balance. It is simply not possible to consult everyone about everything; it would take far too long, cost too much and would be unlikely to result in a different conclusion from a more selective approach. Thus when consultation is necessary, it needs to be organised to facilitate three factors. It should be:

1. *Balanced:* the form of consultation used should be thorough, yet designed to be manageable, not least to be able to do its work in a period of time and in a manner that is appropriate to the task in hand; no sledgehammers to crack nuts.
2. *Representative:* that is if a select group of people are consulted they should be drawn from all the different types of people who will be affected (and who can contribute practically to decision making). In some organisations such selection should accommodate a degree of formality, for example including representatives of staff associations or unions.
3. *Seen to be representative:* perception is important here too: if some, perhaps many, people are *not* going to be consulted individually then they must feel that those who are involved are able to represent all those points of view that are important to the change to be made.

It seems likely therefore that in an organisation of any size that is to move to new premises consultation is important to making everyone feel it is being sensibly handled. I hesitate to use the word fairly as it is often impossible to be strictly fair to everyone. Perhaps a committee is necessary to create a representative group comprising people from all aspects of the organisation's operations. Perhaps that committee's deliberations follow other meetings within different sectors each feeding back information to the main committee which is then responsible for coming to an overall consensus about things.

The purpose of all this is twofold:

1. To maximise acceptance and support for a change by showing that everything everybody would want considered has been considered.
2. To make a practical decision or recommendation: that is one that will make things better for the organisation and those who work for it, rather than one that is based on making it 'fair for everyone'.

The importance of communications is again well illustrated here. People need to know what is being done and understand why it is being done in the way it is, and they also need to accept the premise outlined here that such consultation has not failed if it does not come out with exactly what they would want *personally*. The making of necessary change can in a sense produce winners and losers and, while every effort needs to be made to satisfy everyone and carry them with the development, ultimately the practical realities of the situation need to be understood too. Remember the old saying about omelettes: making them does tend to demand the breaking of eggs.

No stone unturned

These three examples, very different in nature as they are, illustrate the possibilities. Some changes present complex, logistical problems and need sound organisation throughout the process. Other changes may be more of a problem in terms of people and their attitudes. Perhaps the latter are more likely to be overlooked than physical arrangements. For example, the case of moving offices crops up in a Video Arts training film *I wasn't prepared for* (which is actually about presentational skills) and there is a scene that rings all too true when a presentation made to the board is 'recycled' for staff, who are promptly alienated by constant references to the smart offices and parking spaces that will be available for directors. Some aspects of the presentation as it was made to the board should have been replaced when used to inform the wider workforce. Such lapses can occur all too easily.

Every aspect has to be coped with and everything has to be made to go well. The difference between a change well executed and one where poor planning and organisation causes problems will be measured in time and money wasted, people demoralised and reputations and operations diluted in effectiveness.

Action

The complexities involved are well illustrated here and yet are only set out in the context of what makes sense within the pages of a book. Some things are much more complicated, some things are spread across long periods of time and sometimes all the complications come together: something is complex, takes time and may also be contentious. The action here is clear: never underestimate the need for organisation and a systematic approach.

Fit for change

In this chapter we focus on you, the individual. An environment of change affects everyone and what is more the world does not owe you a living. Nor these days can you realistically assume that regular, automatic assistance will be forthcoming from an organisation (if one such employs you) intent on doing everything possible to further your career, or even to assist you to change so that you continue to perform satisfactorily the job you do for it currently. You need to take the initiative and adopt an active approach to personal change, developing your competence to do what you need to be able to do now, and what you want to be able to do in the future. In some ways this may sound obvious and straightforward; however in a busy life, where the workplace tends to be more and more hectic, the tyranny of the urgent can too easily win and such important personal considerations get sidelined. Furthermore it is often necessary to persuade yourself that personal action is really needed: as Leo Tolstoy said, 'Everyone wants to change the world, but no one thinks of changing himself.' If such an approach is undertaken it will help you:

- become more secure in your existing job and role;
- be ready and able to take on new challenges;
- appear an asset to your organisation (and your boss) making you worth developing and promoting on up and through the organisation's structure;
- be desirable in the job market if you choose to move on to another employer;
- obtain fair and satisfactory rewards for what you do (and improve this too if that is an aim).

To a degree, the need for all this is true of every job; everyone needs to be 'career fit', and this is a not a state you achieve and then settle into – it is a moving target, one achieved only after regular ongoing change. This is applicable to anyone working in an organisational environment regardless of age, seniority, gender or experience, and whatever type of industry or kind of organisation they work in. The situations this addresses are widely true across the globe also.

So the focus for the moment is on the individual and thus on individual action: on you and what you can do. We look at how to make what you do, and how you do it, successful; and at how to make it go on being successful over time, so that changes occurring around you do not leave you high and dry.

The danger of change

Even after what has been said in earlier chapters, change may seem a fairly benign word, but it can be almost normal for disaster to stalk the land. Certain industries, like banking, once seemed stable, but they are as subject to difficulties and staff lay-offs as any other sector. Whenever jobs are in jeopardy and when any kind of cull happens a choice must be made. Management does not usually decide to lose the best people; and those who are performing poorly, thought less of or are simply more of an unknown quantity may quickly find themselves (literally) in the firing line.

Essentially this means that people who allow themselves to lag are vulnerable to change. Some minor lag may be no problem when things are going well, but if the lag is significant it may cause problems and certainly if difficult times strike then even a small lag can prove fatal.

This chapter is not designed to help if disaster strikes, but rather to make the chances of that happening to you less likely and, possible disaster apart, to help you excel in a secure, satisfying and rewarding career. But it is certainly also true that being career fit will help you recover if disaster should strike.

The opportunity of change

The very nature of the modern organisational environment means that success is always to be laid primarily at your door; and so too is failure. You have to get things right, and you may get no second chances. And this is as true of your career as it is of your job.

Whatever your expertise at present, it is a fact that its nature and level will need to change. This may mean major extension to your skills portfolio if you are a newcomer to your chosen field, or it may mean what is better described as fine-tuning – though this may still be of considerable significance and influence your ultimate success very much. Whatever it may necessitate, you must ensure that you are always career fit now and at any time in the future.

So, you must ensure such personal change takes place. You must ensure that your knowledge is kept up to date, your expertise and skill continue to be finely tuned and that you are able to do an equally outstanding job tomorrow, next week or next year whatever new circumstances you face.

For someone wanting to become – or remain – successful, inaction is simply not an option. Perhaps we might wish otherwise, but as Beverly Sills said: 'There are no shortcuts to any place worth going.' So it is thus well worth reviewing what makes for effective action in pursuing personal change. As well as providing security and rewards, if your job is going well it tends to be more satisfying too, so changing to keep up to date is also likely to maintain and enhance your job satisfaction.

With the workplace so volatile there are currently few, if any, safe havens, and few, if any, organisations that have remained unaffected. Organisations are always likely to be under pressure and the well-being of their employees is often a lesser goal than sheer survival. All sorts of factors contribute to there being a different work place and work culture than that of the past, including:

- **organisations being under greater market and financial pressure;**
- **changes in the way business and organisations operate (think of the IT revolution or international pressures, for instance);**
- **lower staff numbers and more pressure on individuals;**
- **reduced budgets and thus a reduced ability to fund personal development;**
- **changed terms of employment (think of how the pension schemes offered have changed in the past few years);**
- **more competition between employees to succeed;**
- **higher unemployment;**
- **a general increase in both the amount and speed of change;**
- **the greater likelihood of employers having to take sudden and negative action to protect themselves (such as making people redundant).**

Even a cursory glance at such a list shows that every trend links closely to change. In such an environment there is nothing you can do that will guarantee success (if there ever was). But there are things you can do to make success more likely.

Let us be clear: the focus here is not on finding a job nor even on the whole area of career planning and development in the corporate sense; rather it is about the career enhancement made possible by active personal change to keep you up to date, that is to keep you in a fit state to do your job and succeed in your ongoing career.

For the successful careerist this means a number of things. You must adopt the right attitudes, study and analyse the area and circumstances in which you work, plan and implement action to assist in boosting your competence and thus your progress. You need to be quick on your feet, ready for anything so that you can adjust longer-term plans tactically and fine-tune your actions as necessary. In most, if not all, organisations there is one core process that charts how you are doing and what changes may be necessary to maintain any success you are having: it's the job appraisal process.

Getting the most from job appraisals

This is not the place for me to commend to organisations the merits of a good appraisal system, one that makes a constructive contribution to maintaining and improving performance standards, though it may be worth noting that you are likely to encounter different kinds of appraisal in a career that spans a number of different employers. Not all of them will be effective, some managers are bad at conducting such meetings, and you may not feel all the meetings you experience are constructive. So be it. Careers do not progress in a perfect world, but any appraisal constitutes a major, and potentially career enhancing, form of communication. It is one formal catalyst to change that can act to keep you up to date and make your performance a basis for excellence. You should therefore always seek to get the most from appraisals. Because it is so important to the process of personal change, it is worth including here a 'crash course' on making them effective. This is written from the point of view of the person being appraised, though the points made may well assist appraisers also.

The key issues are fourfold.

1. Appraisals: preparing for them

Be sure you understand how the appraisal system in your
organisation works before you find yourself in such a meeting.
Incidentally, this is a good topic to investigate when you are
being interviewed for a job, but before your first meeting you are
likely to need more detailed information than is spelt out at that
stage. First time round, ask for information and if this is not
provided then ask some of your longer-serving peers how their
meetings go, how long they last and what they get from them.
In particular be sure you know why appraisals are done, how
management conducting them views them, what they look to
get from them, and what time span the review covers.

Then you can consider how you want the meeting to go and
how you can influence it. For instance ask yourself what:

- **you want to raise and discuss;**
- **is likely to be raised (and consider responses to any
  negative areas that may come up);**
- **the link is between appraisal and development and
  training and what you need or hope to get in this area to
  keep you ahead of the game;**
- **the link is between the meeting and your future work,
  responsibilities and projects undertaken;**
- **questions you want to ask.**

If it is not your first appraisal, check what was said at, and
documented after, the last one. This must be done in the context
of what you now know about the forthcoming appraisal meeting.
A couple of points are worth careful planning:

1. One is the link to salary review and other benefits. Many
   organisations separate discussion of this from appraisal
   meetings (indeed there is a strong case for doing so); if
   this is the case then it cannot be raised, except perhaps in
   general terms. If it will be discussed you may have things
   to prepare here also.

2. Another key point is the make up of the discussion in terms of time scale. A good appraisal will always spend more time on the future than on the past (because that is what it aims to influence). Both aspects need thought and certainly there is no excuse for your not having the facts at your fingertips about anything that is a likely candidate for discussion in the review of past events.

Make notes as you plan, and take them with you to the meeting – there is no point in trusting to memory and, in any case, being seen to have thought seriously about the meeting will benefit you. You may only get one, sometimes two, such opportunities in any single year. Therefore, some careful preparation will prevent the occasion being wasted.

2. Appraisals: attending them

The person who is conducting the appraisal will have a bearing on how it is done and how you need to conduct yourself. If it is with a manager with whom you are on good terms and see every day, this will make for a less formal meeting than if it is someone more senior with whom you only have occasional contact (some appraisals involve three or more people including the person to be appraised).

A good appraisal will:

- **be notified well in advance;**
- **have a clear agenda;**
- **allow enough time for the relevant issues to be discussed.**

And so these are things you should ask about if necessary. Particularly you may want to have an idea about how much time will be spent discussing last year and next, how interactive the meeting is and when you can ask questions, perhaps also what is, and is not, on the record. Some appraisals are rather checklist-like in style: that is the appraiser leads the conversation and raises the points one at a time, asking for your view or comment. Others are more open and allow the appraisee to lead, being pulled back to an agenda only if the meeting digresses too much. Ideally you will know which way it runs, but you must be ready for either. Remember, lack of comment may be read as lack of awareness, knowledge or as indecisiveness. On the other hand, if a question posed needs some thought then it is better to let the appraiser know rather than answering with a hasty comment.

Appraisals should not be traumatic occasions. If they are constructive – and prompting change in the future is the only real reason for doing them – then you can take a reasonably relaxed view of them (provided you have done some preparation) and there is no reason why you should not enjoy them and find them useful. You are on show, career planning decisions are being made, albeit long term, by those conducting these meetings, but it is also a positive opportunity for you to present something of your competence in a way that goes 'on the record' (and is usually formally rated, though the details of that are beyond the brief here).

3. Appraisals: the follow-up

Appraisals are too important just to file away in your mind or forget about once they are past. They can provide a catalyst to an ongoing dialogue during the year that will ensure changes set in train maintain momentum and reach their conclusion. In many organisations, the system demands that the appraiser documents proceedings, and usually that the appraisee confirms that this documentation is a true record of the salient issues.

But there is no reason why you cannot take the initiative on particular matters. Consider the following as an example. Development requirements are one topic that most appraisals review. This may result in specific action – I will enrol you on that communication course next month – or it may result in further discussion, more than can be accommodated in the appraisal meeting itself. It may be useful to volunteer to undertake the processes involved (remember, your boss could have a dozen appraisals in the same week and much attendant administration). If you list some suggestions for action, and if this is used as the agenda for another session, then this could well see more of what you plan to happen happening, and happening sooner than would otherwise be the case. Similarly, use the opportunity to report back after any agreed training, in writing or at a meeting, so that the dialogue continues. If the training has been agreed as successful then there is logic in discussing 'what's next?'

A final point: you may think attending them is a chore, but appraisals are not easy to conduct, take time to prepare and always seem to be scheduled during an appraiser's busy periods. So, if it has been useful, express thanks and if it has not, try to comment in a way that may set the scene for a more productive encounter next time.

4. Accept and learn from criticism

A good appraisal is likely to be a good meeting. Even if it is poorly conducted and not really very constructive, it is a satisfying feeling to come out saying to yourself, I did well, particularly when someone else has told you so. But unless you believe the graffiti, which says, I used to be great, but now I am absolutely perfect, few of us get through many such meetings without having to take some criticism. We must consider the possibility that the critical point is fair comment. Face it: you are probably not perfect, you do not get everything right or excel in all you do and you sometimes get things wrong.

Because, perhaps understandably, no one likes having their failures, even minor ones, aired in public there is a danger that you simply put such comment out of your mind and concentrate on the good things that are said (almost all appraisals will touch on both). This may mean you miss opportunities to make positive change. Careers are not enhanced either by repeating mistakes or ignoring failings or weaknesses. If you do not take action to change after an appraisal and do so promptly, at least in terms of planning such action, then the moment will pass. Resolve to take note and, if necessary, action and you will do yourself and your career a favour.

The same principle is true of positive things, so it is equally important to make changes resulting from them; this is no more than the sensible premise of building on success. It too links to skills. For instance if a newly acquired skill is working for you, the next change may be upgrading it so that it can work harder for you.

One key outcome of appraisal is the link to a positive development plan; whether this is designed to change you in a major or minor way, it is important.

Development to change your competence

The ability to handle change is dependent on a variety of approaches as we have seen, but it is also dependent on your capabilities. How you operate draws on your level of knowledge, skills and attitudes that have been developed through your experience to date.

One thing about this is for sure: however competent and up to date you are, the level of your competence must change. Unless you keep up to date in a variety of ways, you will fall behind and your ability not only to handle change but also simply to do your job will be diluted. Development is an ongoing process, and one that is or should be prompted by constructive appraisal. It is possible to regard development as something that the organisation, or your boss, does for you, but it may be better to regard development as a personal responsibility, something that you make happen, rather than something that is wished on you. This is especially true if you want what is then done to assist your performance in the long term rather than simply focus on your current role and responsibilities.

Thus self-development, as we might call it, implies a process directed at change and improvement: to assist you to work better now, but with an eye on the future too; you need to improve specific job performance and thus incorporate or extend the skills that make that possible.

To effectively keep you up to date the development process needs to be:

- **consciously entered into;**
- **well planned;**
- **systematically executed;**
- **focused on clear objectives and intended to make a real and tangible difference.**

Having said that, it should be acknowledged immediately that alongside the specific objectives there are – and should be – more personal and intangible ones, in terms of job satisfaction and career advantage.

In a busy life an activity like self-development must not be a chore, especially not an impossible one, so approaches to it must make it manageable. Certainly in today's work environment spending time on self-development is not just something to do a little of only if time permits: it is a necessity. Your success and future prosperity depends on you changing; the only question is: how much activity is necessary and what should this be?

The answer to this comes, in part, from an understanding and utilisation of the development process.

Getting to grips with the development process

There is no magic formula: many different things can contribute to successful self-development and it is in deciding on the mix of what you do that first influences your ultimate success.

Remember that development can only ever do three things:

1. Change and increase your knowledge: so you can learn about whatever is necessary in your job from background industry knowledge to how your company's product works; both the span and depth of your knowledge matter.
2. Change your skills portfolio: introducing you to new skills and maintaining, improving or refining your abilities in existing ones, dealing with everything from core techniques in something like negotiation to specialist computer skills you may need to deploy.
3. Change attitudes: study can change the way you think about things, although this may take longer than adopting some new skills. For example, something like managing your time effectively is as much a question of the attitude you take to it (and the habits this develops) as of slavishly following techniques. For further information, see *Successful Time Management*, by Patrick Forsyth (Kogan Page).

Next, if your development is going to change anything, two other things must be achieved:

1. You have to set aside some time for self-development. This need not be excessive or unmanageable, but it needs to be there and it needs to be made available on a regular basis.
2. Application is equally important. There is all the difference in the world between skimming through a book, to take a simple example, so that you can say that you have done so, and reading it carefully, studying it over a longer period, making some notes and perhaps also resolving to take some action as a result.

In many jobs the evidence of results, whether good or bad, is clear. Though some development activity may stem from a more general 'look ahead', much of it will come from an examination of the current situation. Managers are charged with monitoring the performance of their staff, and the systematic way that they go about this can equally be applied to oneself.

Consider the formal process, mentioned earlier, first (how your manager might approach it with you in mind). The following four stages can be identified:

1. *Examine the job description:* this allows you to review the levels of knowledge and skills that a particular job demands, and the attitudes required of the person who does it. This states the current ideal and is not, at this stage, linked to the individual presently doing the job.
2. *Examine the person:* this enables a look, alongside the ideal, at what the situation actually is currently. How do the knowledge, skills and attitudes of the individual stack up alongside what the job demands? This information comes from observation of the person, their performance and their results. Formal appraisal is a key part of this, as is other, less formal, evaluation.
3. *Look to the future:* before reaching any conclusions from the process described so far, it is necessary also to think ahead, again focusing on the job rather than the individual. First – change again – what will the job demand in future that will be different from the current situation? What developments – in the organisation, in technology, in the market (affecting competition or the expectation of customers, for instance) and more – are coming? Specifically what new skills, knowledge or attitudes will such changes make necessary, and how will existing ones need to change?
4. *Defining the gap:* together two factors coming from the above may define a gap – the combination of any shortfall in current levels of competence plus the need to add to this for the future, which is the so-called development (or training) gap and describes the area towards which development must be directed by any individual.

Of course, the picture produced may be fine; no immediate action may be necessary. In so dynamic an environment, the reality at any particular moment is most likely that some action – major or minor – is, in fact, necessary (or will be). If so a plan of action is needed to deal with implementation. Again viewing this systematically provides a simple checklist approach as to what you need to do:

- **List what needs to be addressed: whatever is identified, from minor matters that need only a small input to the development of new skills that must be approached from square one.**
- **Rate the list in terms of priorities: in most organisations resources, that is time (including yours), money and the availability of training and facilities, are finite. It is unlikely to be possible to do everything that might be desirable instantly, and impossible to select what comes first or should be postponed without asking which changes rank as priorities.**
- **Put some timing to it: having established priorities you need to consider when things are to be done: what is urgent? What can be postponed without causing problems and what might be addressed in parts? (Perhaps with something being done early on, but action also planned to follow up and complete the training task later – an approach that might make it easier to sell to a manager.)**
- **Consider the most suitable method: this factor needs to relate quite closely to timing. With a list of desirable development activities and priorities set, the next thing is to consider exactly how something will be approached (a course, a project, whatever).**
- **Calculate costs: this is always an important issue, and realistically may involve some compromise and a balancing of different approaches; when you are initiating things the question of who is to pay needs considering – you or the organisation.**
- **Link to an action plan: the net result of all these deliberations needs to be documented, and turned into**

a rolling plan that sets out what will be done, in what way, when and who will be involved.

Methods of development

The fourth point – consider the most suitable method – is worth elaborating a little. Attendance on courses may be a prime method for development that springs to mind. Fine, it often is, though it demands more than passive observance. Attending a course should make you think, it should be hard work and especial effort is necessary to ensure that change really does follow attendance. Think about what you may attend, what it will offer and how you will conduct yourself; make some notes and plan to get as much as possible from it whatever form it may take. Indeed review all the possible training methods that might help (see the box below).

Training methods
These include the following:

- **Activity courses: much used for developing teamwork and leadership, these place great emphasis on informal learning; extreme versions can have you improvising to complete such tasks as crossing a river with nothing to assist you but a football, a custard tart and a ball of string.**
- **Simulations: here technology lends a hand and development takes the form of working on a usually computer-based 'game'; one that creates a case designed for instance to show the interaction of competitors in a market.**
- **Packaged training: this term encompasses a range of programmes using computers, CDs, DVDs and more,**

and involving an element of interaction as you progress through the material; such can often be undertaken on a solo basis (and can be efficient too: a CD might be played in the car while commuting).

- Open learning: while 'packaged training' is normally self-contained, open learning implies a link from this sort of kit to a tutor and with the added facility of an input from outside to enhance the material.
- Resource centres: these are often the preserve of larger companies: a library facility and beyond that the provision of a range of developmental materials and equipment. Here someone can go and watch a video, spend time at a dedicated computer learning station, engage in certain small group activities – or just find a helpful book or a word of advice.
- Job rotation and swapping: with this (used by comparatively few organisations) people are intentionally moved into new jobs, rather different to what they were doing previously, for developmental reasons.
- Secondment: for some a good, and convenient, way of developing people is to post them for longer or shorter periods away from their present location. This may simply be to a branch office (or from a branch to headquarters); or to a location where activity is specialised: a research facility perhaps or even somewhere overseas.
- Films: training films cover a range of topics well, especially personal skills ranging from selling and negotiating to time management, and all the major providers have catalogues and websites you can check out. Films (and the manuals that accompany them) do not offer complete training in a moment – that would be unrealistic – but they do offer good encapsulations of principles and illustrate matters in a memorable way (or the good ones do).

- **Sabbaticals: these, often linked to reward for long service, are a period of paid leave during which development activities may be a part; being away from operational pressures may allow longer or different activities to be scheduled.**

Simpler methods may be just as useful. Reading this book is an example, so would be resolving to read a business book each month, choosing well and sticking to the commitment. A complete list of methods is neither possible here nor is it intended, but what is listed reminds one of the range of possibilities and all may link to change in the way that has been described.

It is worth putting yourself in a position to check, quickly and regularly, what is possible, what is new and what else you can do. Leave no stone unturned in seeking ways to stay up to date: for example it may also be worthwhile to:

- subscribe to various trade and business journals, and those specific to the function and role in which you work;
- subscribe to relevant newsletters, e-zines and suchlike delivered automatically to your computer;
- allow your name to be added to certain mailing lists (for instance to get news of the latest products from a training film company whose preview meetings you might attend);
- occasionally (regularly?) attend relevant exhibitions (for example a trade show to improve competitor intelligence or a training exhibition to see what new development aids might be available and useful); ditto trade or functional conferences;
- cultivate a friend in the HR department (or similar) especially if you are in a large organisation, or indeed

anyone else for that matter who can give you access to useful information.

All activity designed to make you more effective in your job and to change and boost your competence is worthwhile. So too can anything that will act to make it happen (for instance the technique of mentoring referred to on pages 91). For instance, formal schemes to ensure ongoing development takes place are provided by many professional bodies in the form of CPD (continuing professional development) schemes like the one operated by a body of which I am a member, the Chartered Institute of Marketing. Any prompt to regular change is worthwhile. Consider the options here carefully. Some things can be adopted on a regular basis; undertaking them can become a positive habit. Other things are more occasional, or one-off, and everything must be assessed regularly to see if it is still useful or if your mix of development activity should contain something else instead.

In this kind of way training and development activities can be considered, worked out and scheduled on a basis that makes sense. Such consideration must:

- **relate closely to current operational matters;**
- **relate also to specific anticipated changes;**
- **allow you to link and liaise as necessary with your line manager and also any appropriate central department or manager (e.g. a training manager) – not least to draw on their experience and expertise.**

The personal implications are clear: whatever management may do, you need to think things through in a similar way and you need a written 'personal change plan' – one that you can roll forward and fine-tune over time. Starting from scratch preparing such a plan may take a few minutes, and keeping it up to date and monitoring progress need not take long (the plan might well be one sheet of paper, though make sure what you write is sufficient to make sense when looked at some months later).

Usually such a plan will have most of the detail for the next three or six months then become more of an outline listing only a proportion of what it is planned will happen. The process is manageable; certainly it is wholly worthwhile in terms of the results you will get from it as you implement what it prescribes.

Analyse and update yourself

Here we concentrate on the personal aspects for a moment, first overall and then with regard to specific challenges. It is not enough to keep up to date in the ways described; you must also be seen in the right light. People must know you are keeping up to date and must appreciate the competence that this gives you. To be ready and able to make changes and progress in your career you need to have certain thinking done and certain action taken; not least you need to be seen to be keeping up with change. Some examples follow.

CVs

The curriculum vitae (CV) is a document everyone should have on file. Not only should you have one, you should keep it up to date. Make a note on your file copy about any events (particularly successes) that need adding and about anything that needs deleting or replacing with something more appropriate; then on a regular basis, perhaps a couple of times each year, rework it. Remember too that a CV is not a standard document; it must record the changes going on in your career, show that you can and do change and also perhaps that you are an agent for change. If you need to use it, to apply for a new job say, then you first need to review it and tailor it appropriately, emphasising those things that might appeal to a particular potential employer. The same applies to covering letters designed to accompany CVs.

Watch the job market

If you are at a stage when you have decided that moving on is the right way forward, then do so well informed. The job market changes all the time. Regular observation will allow you to choose when and how to act and make sure that you miss no opportunities.

Watch and liaise internally too

New opportunities (and dangers) can open up internally and so you need to take notice of your surroundings, network and generally be aware of changes, developments and possible opportunities.

Check how you are perceived

Whatever your level of self-confidence is, and even if you feel you are obviously doing well or destined for the top, you should work at presenting the right profile and characteristics (from competence to being approachable) to the work place and to the world. With that in mind you need to make sure that you:

- **Look the part: power dressing may be inappropriate and prevailing styles change so it is not possible to be didactic here, though you should appear smart and things like clean shoes and fingernails, and well-cut hair may be worth worrying about.**
- **Act the part: by this I mean looking professional and organised; a tidy desk might be good and certainly arriving late for a meeting with papers spilling out of an overfilled file is not likely to instantly label you efficient.**
- **Have external visibility: even if you are not (yet) the organisation's spokesperson on radio or television,**

there may be visibility to be created through company newsletters, committee work, writing articles or more.

- Cooperate: a willingness to cooperate is usually seen as good; most organisations prefer team players to rogue individuals (appropriate socialising is part of this).
- Avoid being typecast: your job will doubtless involve different things, and that difference will change as time goes by. You need to be seen as operating right for now and in the future, not stuck in a time warp.

Action

Two things are important here: deciding the profile you want and actively working at putting it over; this involves a wide range of activity from how you make a presentation to how you deal with others.

Achievement and results

As a further thought in this chapter let's link what has been said to one overriding factor: the achievement of targeted results. There is only one, but strong, message to bear in mind here. It is a truism that you should never confuse activity with achievement. For the most part, the opportunities in corporate life come largely from achieving what is required of you. Looking busy, being busy, having (and surmounting) difficulties, succeeding with peripheral matters with which no one else seems to bother, none of these are as important as meeting your main objectives.

So, perhaps the most important rule here is this: successfully achieving your goals or targets (whatever form they take) is of first importance in building your career; indeed it is the foundation

of everything else you do. Attention to this is a prerequisite and, although many other matters as we have seen need attention to keep you up to date, the effectiveness of all of them is reduced, perhaps drastically reduced, by any failure of achievement.
On the other hand it is a dangerous trap to feel that provided you are achieving successfully all is well and no further action is necessary. Even competent people can be overlooked and real shrinking violets are in most danger of this – at worst, if you look like a doormat then people will tend to walk all over you. And remember that while things are going well the need for change remains; indeed its ongoing necessity can easily get overlooked. So perhaps when matters are going well that is precisely the time to give change some thought.

Agent for change

The combination of being up to date in every way necessary, being seen to be so and also achieving what you are charged with and making sure that people know this, enables you to survive and thrive in the dynamic conditions of the twenty-first century. Only if you are on top of things in this way will you be in a position to initiate changes of your own. Now we consider a number of 'change challenges'. There can be many and they will vary over time and for each individual, but the 20 picked here will affect most readers.

20 challenges demanding change

At this stage let's start by going back to a point made early on. Change seems to engender instant negative feelings; many people are much more likely to find that their instinctive reaction to coming change is fear of what the negative effects may be, especially personally, rather than the reverse. But it is better to regard the glass as half full. Let us be clear, many changes prove to:

- **have fewer negative effects than you first think;**
- **lead on to positive effects and even opportunities for you;**
- **allow you to influence, and if necessary mitigate, the effect on you.**

Perhaps the third listed is the most important to get to grips with. If positive change comes then the only job is to take advantage of it, and if any fears you have prove to be unfounded that is good. Reacting to change though needs a positive approach and also some consideration and analysis. As it said on the cover of *The Hitchhikers' Guide to the Galaxy* – 'don't panic'; it's good advice. Any change needs a reasoned approach to it and with any change that is thrust upon you, step back, think it through and act in the best possible way. Not least you are then likely to make it through the change better than those that do panic.

Consider the kind of things many are likely to face in future; the challenges to come will doubtless be many and varied, but the following 20 (which are not presented in any order of priority or to exclude other things) are certainly things many readers will face; and, despite dangers, all can potentially benefit you.

1. *Technological (IT) change:* this has already been mentioned and is ongoing; it will happen, or rather continue. We all have to spend time keeping up in this area. It is possible. You need to expect it so take time to check it out. Take advice, for instance from an organisation's IT specialists and always ask questions if necessary (struggling on is just likely to see you get further behind). Of course some change has negative effects and we can all think of computer systems that drive us mad (probably in ways that their originators did not intend) but few would want to go back to a pre-computer way of operating.

2. *Communications:* communications is communications surely. But this too is an area of change – witness the sometimes ludicrous spectacle of someone emailing a colleague who is sitting a couple of paces away. On the

one hand you need to fit in with prevailing ways (for instance a boss may want things done a particular way); on the other hand even as you accommodate change remember that clarity is always the most important thing in communication however that communication may travel.

3. *Moving offices:* this happens from time to time, often for positive reasons (growth demands more space) and if there are negative effects then they need a logical approach. For instance, moaning about where your workplace will be is unlikely to cut much ice – everyone will have concerns – but practical considerations, for instance linked to communications, may help.

4. *New colleagues:* such could be a threat, but don't take only that view – get to know them, exchange information and perhaps even swap tasks, form alliances, and help incorporate them into the team. By all means remain vigilant, but a positive attitude is essential here. As it is with the ...

5. *New boss:* of course this is a worry, but it is also an opportunity. People are all different and so things that have been blocked may now be approved and it is a chance to show what you can do. Concentrate on areas of skill or task that you want to develop and see how far you can go. Remember that the relationship you have with a boss is not preordained; you need to work at creating it and recognise that as much of how it is comes from you as from the boss.

6. *Lower staff levels:* this is always worrying and there is probably no guarantee in today's turbulent world against hitting problems. Being forewarned is forearmed, as they say, is the key: do a good job, keep up to date, attend to development, communications, your relationship with your boss and others and you will remain fit to survive, indeed to thrive. I have written at more length about all of this in *Disaster Proof Your Career* (Kogan Page).

7. *Changed role:* a change of role or activity may be thrust upon you. It could be you want to fight this, though be sure

that you do (it may be a lost cause); more likely the problem here is a transient one. It may be different, it may be a challenge, but it could well lead on to a new – and improved – circumstance. I know that when I set up my own operation in 1990 it seemed very daunting (though I was choosing to do so) but I quickly came to regard it as the best career decision I ever made; albeit it took some working at.

8. *Increased responsibility:* like a larger job change (see number 7) this is sometimes daunting, but can almost always lead on to better things. You need to rise to the challenge and give it a fair chance, but also make sure that you are suitably equipped to take on whatever is necessary. Do not be afraid to ask – a briefing, some training, a mentor, all sorts of things can help bridge the gap and it may be up to you to take the initiative and get such things organised.

9. *New skills:* you need to extend your skills; it is part of the overall process of keeping up. But you also need to actively develop skills. My first published book is long out of print – thank goodness. If writing it taught me anything it was that I needed to learn a good deal more about the craft of writing. It needed an active approach (some training and a good mentor) and some practice, but I improved. I have still to write the great novel but I make a good proportion of my income writing, so I must have moved forward. It is just the same if you find you must start writing reports, negotiating or much else.

10. *Breadth of vision:* one of the differences that is necessary as you rise through an organisation is that by and large more senior roles demand a wider perspective. This means you must keep more balls in play, work over a longer time span and see, and accommodate, the broad effects of actions in how you work. This is quite a change and, if you aim to move on and up, you need to move towards this ahead of actually needing it.

11. *Creativity:* another area that goes with increased seniority is that of creativity. More senior managers must spend

more time seeking new ways forward – essentially initiating change – rather than just maintaining, however effectively, on-going activities. Again this is an approach to recognise and get to grips with ahead of actually needing it.

12. *Self-sufficiency:* one of the work trends that will make a change for many people is what might be summarised as 'increased pressure' (fewer staff, money and pressure on resources all contribute to this). The effect I want to mention here is that there is less support, less training and less management time for people. If you are to make progress then more of the initiative must come from the individual. While you need to organise things, it does give you a new element of control – you decide what you want to push for and, provided you make a good case for it, there is no reason why this change cannot help you.

13. *Numbers:* performance will in future be even more under the microscope than in the past: more targets, financial and otherwise will be the norm. This is fair enough in some respects (everything possible must be done to ensure results are achieved), but it may demand more than passive acceptance. You may need to be able to fight your corner and negotiate such targets and you may need a higher level of numeracy than in the past to let you understand and do this. That said the employees that deliver will continue to thrive.

14. *Work–life balance:* this is certainly an area of change. The nature of families, and not least of their finances, means that ways of working must fit with the complexities of a range of factors from childcare to housing; and such things change constantly. Personal organisation is necessary to get a good fit here. Pressurised employers are, rightly or wrongly, unlikely to see it as their job to accommodate such factors to any great extent; certainly you should not expect this. You may well need to adapt at home and be persuasive and flexible at work to achieve the right balance.

15. *Restrictions:* there seem to be a plethora – and an increasing number – of rules and regulations that an

organisation must comply with. Health and safety is just one area; other rules, procedures and, let's be honest, red tape combine to create an ongoing need to maintain efficiency. However much some of this may be necessary, it all certainly puts a premium on those who have the ability to streamline operations. Accommodating such changes as they affect both individuals and organisations provides an opportunity for some people.

16. *Pace:* it is said that the pace of change has never been faster; perhaps this is true – until tomorrow. Here the need for those initiating or involved in change is to react fast but continue to do so in a considered fashion. There is an old saying to the effect that if you decide in haste, you may repent at leisure. Living in a changing world requires you to balance things here – juggling speed with a considered and effective approach. Again there are opportunities for those adopting this approach.

Alongside the factors picked so far I would add a few examples of more overall, corporate factors:

17. *Competition:* challenges in the market and not least international competition (consider the rise of China as just one example) mean that everything from product development to marketing must constantly be striving to anticipate competitive pressures and stay ahead in a dynamic market. This increases the need for change and also the pace of change across a range of activities.

18. *Corporate reorganisation:* one of the impacts of competition and market pressure is that more organisations change their structure and organisation. Takeovers, mergers and the like almost always generate a worrying period and realistically do not benefit everyone. This tendency stresses the importance of keeping up and remaining 'fit for purpose' in a work context – it also creates an opportunity to change things within the new structure. New owners may as much seek guidance from existing employees as unthinkingly

change the way things work (which they may anyway not yet sufficiently understand). It is a situation that contains opportunities amidst difficulties.

19. *Distribution:* the way companies relate to their markets is also subject to change with such factors as the rise of the internet, the decline of the high street and much, much more all combining to give organisations a good deal to think about. Here too change must be coped with but individuals also need to initiate the response to all this.

Finally let's return to changes you may want:

20. *Greener grass:* the grass may not always be greener elsewhere, whether you define that as working differently or in a whole new area. But there may be changes you want: to work in the New York office, to be on the board, to travel more (or less), whatever – not quite anything may be possible, but things you do not push for will probably not occur. Remember that many changes need your active initiation.

The moral here is simple: think things through. Ask:

- **Exactly what is going to happen?**
- **What are the likely positive effects and how can you take advantage of them?**
- **What – objectively – are the negatives, if any?**
- **Are they really negatives?**
- **If there are can they be reduced?**
- **What action do you need to take promptly or at a later date?**
- **Would it be useful to set out an action plan?**

If the answer to the last point is yes, then make a written note of what you need to do, take action and monitor and adjust the process if necessary as you go ... and always think positive and keep an image in mind of that glass being half full as you do so.

Action

Always remember that change affects you – how you plan your future and how you act in a variety of circumstances will always be important and will need an active approach to ensure success in your work and career.

Afterword

As this text has surely shown, change is important, necessary and ongoing. Despite this it is not always easy to instigate change and doing so can be downright difficult. Even simple, perhaps that should be written as 'simple', changes can be uncertain and major ones can be challenging and risk much if they are not made or are made late or inexpertly executed.

Amongst the portfolio of skills a manager needs to be successful and progress in their career, the ability to recognise the need for change and to set out to instigate changes and implement the process successfully is surely an important one. If you are early in your career and have escaped this so far, the likelihood is that you will meet change management sooner or later. As this book has made clear you need to be an agent of change and see yourself, what you know, the competencies, skills and attitudes you bring to bear on the job, as dynamic too. In life, scientists tell as that virtually every cell in our bodies is replaced every seven years or so. We are, all of us, literally not the same person that we were seven years ago. This happens without you even thinking about it; the changes discussed here do not happen automatically, but changes do need to be made. You will not be the same manager in

a few years' time, but make the right changes and you will find
you are a better one.

Key questions

As a final checklist below is a series of questions that you can use
either to assess how well something already executed was done or
to assess the way you plan to make a future change and make sure
that it is successful. These are arranged broadly chronologically
and divided into logical stages; all rate yes/no answers.

DEFINITION: what is to be changed?

- **Have you defined clearly what situation needs
  either overcoming (problems) or exploiting
  (opportunities)?**
- **Is the focus right (for instance is it on root causes
  rather than just on the symptoms of a problem)?**
- **Have suitable levels of consultation been involved in
  arriving at a clear definition of the change to be
  made?**
- **Do those involved understand and agree the
  situation?**

OUTCOMES: what is to be achieved?

- **Have objectives defining what will be different after
  the change is made been clearly stated?**
- **Is there a clear and satisfactory link with overall
  corporate goals?**
- **Again, have these issues been discussed, understood
  and agreed by all concerned?**
- **Is there a means in place to measure success?**

COMMITMENT: are people in favour?

- Do people not simply understand and agree, but actively support the change and what it involves?
- Have any doubts they express been addressed?
- Is there suitable, powerful, senior support in place?

STAKEHOLDERS: are all such informed and committed?

- Have all potential and actual stakeholders been identified?
- Have appropriate consultation and communication been undertaken with all involved? (If necessary this must involve different processes for different groups.)
- Has feedback from this process been accommodated and any doubts addressed?
- Is their agreement and support in place?
- Are they positively motivated regarding the change?

METHODOLOGY: how will things be done?

- Is the kind of change well described? (For instance, innovative or strategic.)
- Does the methodology chosen for use in implementation match the nature of the change?
- Has how things will happen been well communicated?
- Is the expertise of those involved (good or bad) allowed for in the implementation planning?
- Are you content the implementation methods are well chosen and will work?

IMPLEMENTATION: an action plan for change

- Is there a (written) action plan specifying exactly how the implementation will proceed?

- Does it specify *what* will be done, *who* will do it and *by when* it is scheduled to take place?
- Is there someone clearly 'wearing the change implementation hat' to oversee the whole process?
- Are regular ongoing operations safeguarded during the process of change?
- Are all concerned well informed?

MEASUREMENT: how will success be measured?

- Are measurement processes in place?
- Do they monitor progress during implementation (in order to allow fine-tuning) as well as success at the conclusion?
- Do elements of measurement link to the future so that later change programmes can learn from this one?

LOOKING AHEAD: ongoing review

- Are regular procedures in place to spot the need or opportunity of future changes and feed such information into operations?

The answer to all such questions should be yes. The above questions are chosen to illustrate the process, but such a list, in tailored form, may form a useful checklist in your planning for any specific future change.

In addition, and to emphasise the last heading in the box above, perhaps you occasionally – regularly – need to ask what areas within your organisation have not been changed for a while and might benefit from review. There is an old saying – if it ain't broke, don't fix it – but perhaps in this era of change the opposite is worth a thought – if it ain't broke, break it, and then make it better. Change is not only a reaction to the changing environment around you – in future it is likely to be those organisations seeking out opportunities for positive change that succeed best. And that means working at it. Sometimes change is one jump from here to there; sometimes it is a series of steps. It is an oft-used phrase that we should 'not keep reinventing the wheel', but one can look further back for a story and a lesson:

It is said that the wheel was not invented in a flash of creative brilliance; like everything else it initially had certain bugs and these took time for Stone Age man to sort out. The very first wheels, the product of the innovative Kwik-trip Korporation, were, in fact, square in shape. They did beat carrying heavy things, but only just – and they gave a somewhat bumpy ride. Customers bought them, well exchanged them as money hadn't been invented yet, but they also complained. Ug, who was in charge of new product development at KtK, thought long and hard about possible changes. Then he had an idea.

He set to work and made a new batch of wheels incorporating his idea. When one of his best customers arrived a few days later he proudly showed off his latest innovation. 'A change for the better,' said Ug. But his customer was not immediately enthusiastic: 'How on earth is that better?' he said. 'It's triangular!'

'That's right!' he was told enthusiastically. 'One less bump!'

The moral here is clear: a number of steps may be involved to get where you want; in which case each one must be made with due care, but sometimes also a great leap is the only way.

To end, let's reiterate two points. First you must recognise that making change and making it successfully is not necessarily easy. You cannot instigate change just by snapping your fingers and shouting, 'All change now!' What is necessary is a careful, planned and systematic approach with every detail well worked out and implementation designed to be effective in creating the desired results and, not least, to carry people – preferably happily – with it.

Secondly, though we might sometimes feel that change is what we want *other* people do, make no mistake, change *is* the order of the day. It is not an option. If you work in an organisation that wants to survive and thrive, and indeed if you want to do so yourself, then you must cope with it, and it is best to embrace its necessity and view it positively. I would go further: success in future will go primarily to those who not only deal effectively with change but *who also actively seek it out.* Because it is the changes that are made then that are likely to be most important and have the greatest impact on future success.

I surely cannot put it better than management guru Tom Peters, who said:

> *Life is pretty simple: You do some stuff. Most fails. Some works. You do more of what works. If it works big, others quickly copy it. Then you do something else. The trick is the doing something else.*

Doing something else – that is a philosophy which in these dynamic times we must surely all embrace.